LOUISA CALDER'S
CREATIVE CROCHET

Louisa Calder, wife of sculptor Alexander Calder, has crocheted for most of her life. Her husband, one of the greatest sculptors of all time, was responsible for the first true revolution in the history of sculpture – by giving it a completely new dimension: movement.

Louisa Calder with her work, published for the first time in this book, has added a new dimension to crochet – elevating it from the narrow confines of a craft in danger of becoming moribund to an art – an art of tremendous vitality, creativity and freedom.

Mary Konior, crochet specialist and teacher, discusses, analyses and explains in the introduction Louisa Calder's work, opening up new vistas for both experienced crochet workers and beginners.

With the detailed instructions covering all facets of crochet, this is also an everyday handbook.

LOUISA CALDER'S
CREATIVE CROCHET

by
LOUISA CALDER
and
MARY KONIOR

A STUDIO BOOK
THE VIKING PRESS · NEW YORK

This book was designed and produced by
Park and Roche Establishment, Schaan

Design: Bob Hook
House Editor: Vicki Robinson

First published 1979

Copyright © Park and Roche Establishment, 1979

All rights reserved

ISBN 0 670 44203 8

Set in Monophoto Univers
Printed in Italy by
Amilcare Pizzi, SA, Milan

CONTENTS

INTRODUCTION

"I like using a simple stitch and a simple design with bright
colours. My aim in this book is to stimulate rather than
teach, and to encourage people to use their imagination."

Louisa Calder

Louisa Calder's work gives an instant impression of tremendous vitality and creativity. Colourful abstract shapes romp over the surface of her crochet like children at play. For her crochet is an art form more than a traditional craft. "Anyone can create in crochet," she says.

The simplicity of the fabric structure allows her free play with colour, resulting in exuberant geometric shapes evocative of twentieth-century painting. Many of her designs are based on rectangular shapes with further interplay of square, rectangular or linear form, in stimulating full strength colours. The striped and banded element which characterises her work results from the technique of working crochet in straight rows or in spiral rounds.

Her designs have the advantage that pattern instructions do not need to be set down in the traditional manner. The usual row upon row of abbreviated stitch directions, often tedious to use, require to be followed to the letter and deter many an aspiring beginner. The patterns are given as explanations rather than as definitive working instructions, and the illustrations speak clearly for themselves. The designs are so easy to understand that a beginner of any age can work from them with ease as soon as the main stitch, double crochet (American single crochet) has been mastered. Children can often manage this stitch from about the age of seven years old, and some of Louisa Calder's small purse designs are very suitable as mother and child projects. Her ideas can be used as a basis for variations on a theme or they can be copied. The variety of creative designs possible in the manner she has pioneered is limited only by the worker's imagination and energy.

The ideas contained in this book can, with a little practice, be extended to many more ambitious projects. Once the basic skills have been mastered, it should be easy for the reader to design a great variety of garments and objects not necessarily illustrated here.

Louisa Calder creates by eye, building up an interplay of shapes and colours as she progresses. She finds it unnecessary to plan to the smallest detail beforehand as she has an excellent "seeing eye" reinforced by years of living in an artistic environment. However, there is no reason why the design should not be planned first if preferred, as double crochet (American single crochet) designs can be plotted like tapestry designs on squared graph paper.

A design should be interesting and engage attention, and Louisa Calder's refreshing attitude is to allow any imperfection in workmanship to work for the design – to give it additional interest. Her advice is to use deliberately any occurrence which might traditionally have been regarded as an imperfection, if it enhances the final result. For instance, when changing colours along a row, many of her repeating shapes have a little echo of colour running into the background. Once, this would have been regarded as a technical fault, but she maintains, quite rightly, that the little echo adds interest to a simple shape, like an exclamation mark or speech accent.

The Craft of Crochet

Hand-produced textiles can be classified as single thread or multi-thread techniques. The single thread group which includes crochet and knitting has one continuous thread which can be traced throughout the work. This is so even when several coloured threads are employed, as only one of them is "in production" at one time.

The multi-thread techniques, which include weaving and macramé, require a number of threads to be pre-cut and set up either on a warp or on bobbins before work can start. The fact that crochet needs no preliminary setting up is a great advantage and is one of the reasons for its popularity. Another advantage of the single continuous thread of both crochet and knitting is that it can be unravelled quickly and easily, although conversely this may be considered a disadvantage. The multi-thread techniques are troublesome to unravel.

The basic action of producing crochet is very simple and works on the principle of one loop of thread being pulled through another. All crochet stitches without exception are varying permutations of this action. Fingers alone are sufficient of a tool to pull loops through each other, and finger crochet is worth trying just to get the feel of the initial impetus which must have given birth to the craft in pre-historic times, as well as for the sheer fascination of playing with thread. The index finger of the right hand is used as a hook. Erratic tension has to be acceptable if the method is to be put to practical use, because however dainty the finger it is still a clumsy hook.

The basic action of looping one thread through another can also be achieved with a non-hooked instrument, or more practically with a pair of knitting needles. Knitting and crochet are interrelated and are usually assumed to have had a common origin. This origin, technically a cross between the two methods, is now known as Tunisian Crochet (in America as Afghan Crochet), as well as by a variety of other names including those of German, and Tricot Crochet. Once upon a time it was described as Shepherd's Knitting, giving a fanciful vision of working straight from the fleece, but the term is now obsolete. To work Tunisian Crochet, an extra long hook is needed with a knob on the end, in order to hold a row of partially worked crochet stitches which are held all at once like knitted stitches.

Before the technique of knitting became finalised on pointed needles, it evidently went through a stage when it was worked on hooked needles, and any knitter in search of amusement is recommended to try knitting on two crochet hooks in order to appreciate its manual development. Stitches do not drop although progress is slow. It would seem that the permutations and combinations of related craft techniques are considerable, and there is a great deal of scope for research.

The word "crochet" is French and means hook, so that by definition any craft work produced with the aid of a hook can be described as crochet. Several other languages use a name equivalent to "hookwork". In the very widest sense of the meaning, the term "crochet" can be used to cover the present-day hook crafts of hairpin work, tambour work and hooked rugs.

The difference in contemporary American and British terms for crochet stitches has arisen because crochet was introduced into America by continental European settlers rather than by early British settlers.

The Historical Development of Crochet

The exact beginnings of crochet as a manual skill are unknown. Logically one would guess that finger crochet came first, as this would quickly have followed the discovery of spinning which occurred very early in the dawn of civilisation. It then needed the idea of using a hooked implement to replace and improve on the fingers. The first primitive hooks were bone harpoon-type spears used for hunting and fishing, and it is easy to imagine an erstwhile crafty lady appropriating her man's hunting hook for her own purposes.

It had always been assumed that the crafts of crochet and knitting were an invention of the early middle eastern Arabian civilisations judging from remnants discovered in archaeological excavations, but this theory is no longer totally acceptable since both crochet and knitting have been discovered in ethnic studies in South America, where they had evidently developed quite independently since they differ from any European technique.

Traditional crochet, or the techniques generally classed under this heading, that is the full range of known stitches in ornate structural combinations, often with a raised surface and openwork background, developed during the sixteenth century as an alternative method of producing lace, at a time in European history when there was a good deal of interest in lace making and in lace wearing. Until this time, the craft of crochet had remained relatively undeveloped, having been worked with homespun yarns and with the use of wooden and bone hooks. It was plain and rather coarse work and could be described as peasant or cottage crochet. Very little is known of its technical detail but it is probable that the methods used were Tunisian Crochet and the "beginner's" stitch, double crochet (American single crochet).

With the availability of fine linen lace threads, it required only a lacemaker's hook suitable for the handling of very fine threads, and crochet could take on a dainty lacelike quality. This further development is attributed entirely to the painstaking work of nuns, particularly in the large convents of Southern Europe. So much of the history of crochet is conjecture, but, again, it is possible to imagine a nun, struggling with too-fine a thread in a dim convent light, intending to work the usual double crochet (American single crochet) and getting her threads tangled on the hook, as often happens with crochet threads, thus producing a "wrong" double crochet (American single crochet) of twice its intended length, and being wise enough to recognise the potential use of this longer stitch. The treble stitch (American double crochet) must have been discovered accidentally in this way, and once it was seen to be a valuable aid to fine crochet, a whole range of complicated and ornamental stitch arrangements depending directly on the use of the treble (American double crochet) would have followed very quickly.

These intricate crochet techniques were developed during the lace wearing ages as a method of copying designs then in use for needlepoint and bobbin laces. The influence of many old lace designs is still apparent in traditional crochet. Torchon lace, which is an easily recognised bobbin lace characterised by a diamond shaped mesh, was accurately and extensively copied on the hook, resulting in an equally easily recognised style of crochet. The popular square block designs of Filet Crochet were inspired by the earlier embroidered Filet Guipure laces. Irish Crochet, the finest and most intricate of all crochet work, originated as a copy of Venetian Rose Point, a richly ornate needlepoint lace featuring raised rosettes and scrolls. Later on, many Maltese and Cluny bobbin lace designs were faithfully copied in crochet. The main reason for crochet copies of the lace originals was that of speed; crochet was, and still is, a much quicker method of lace production than bobbin or needlepoint methods.

However, original design and genuine creativity are very much inhibited by the fact that traditional crochet designs are derivative. It is as though this type of work has been developed to its limits, and the only means of progress for crochet now is a return to its origin, back to the simplicity of drawing a loop through a loop, in order to discover a different direction. Its craft potential has been fully exploited but its artistic potential has only just begun to be recognised and appreciated.

It is interesting to note that there have been recent attempts to revitalise the craft of bobbin lace. A few contemporary workers of bobbin lace are reverting to the origins of their own craft and discovering non-traditional ways of development. However, it would be ridiculous if the rebirth of crochet were to imitate the rebirth of bobbin lace, just because traditional crochet once imitated traditional bobbin lace.

The future progress of crochet promises to be exciting and very far removed from the traditions of the craft. Research is proving that all the textile fabrics can be used to give shape and meaning to thread. A good deal of investigation is taking place in America, especially in the art schools of California, where crochet has long been appreciated as an art form. The movement is towards the creation of three-dimensional abstract and figurative sculptural constructions often featuring unexpected threads both natural and man-made. Any fibre that will withstand the pull of a hook is being drawn into use. The hollow forms produced by the technique of working crochet spirally in rounds are frequently stuffed and shaped as soft sculptures. The larger works are supported on armatures.

Following the contemporary general interest in and revival of all the textile crafts, and with the relaxation of traditional rules and the broader concept of art forms, there is a tendency towards the combination of different craft processes in the same work. Crochet can be successfully combined with a variety of other techniques. It mixes especially well with weaving and tapestry as well as with the more obvious knitting and hooked rug techniques. In fact a patchwork construction can be built up from any mixture which will give substance to an idea.

Designing with Colour

A well-developed intuitive colour sense is usually regarded with envy as a Good Fairy's Gift at the cradle side. Those who have been so luckily endowed can just reach out for a coloured yarn, but most of us need a little guidance.

There are several complex and involved colour theories, and as an area of study the subject is fraught with difficulty because of the use of conflicting vocabularies. Some theories relate to the solar spectrum, some to painter's pigments, and others to the psychology of vision.

The three primary colours are red, yellow and blue, the three secondary colours are mixtures of the primaries: red plus yellow gives orange, yellow plus blue gives green, blue plus red gives violet. These six are often illustrated as a circle of colours in rainbow sequence, showing red opposite to green, yellow opposite to violet, and blue opposite to orange. Colours which are opposite in such a colour circle are called complementary colours, and when mixed they neutralise each other and produce grey.

Any pure colour can be modified by being darkened to deeper shades or lightened to paler tints. Each of these gradations of colour can be further modified or neutralised by the addition of a complementary colour. If the main colour chosen for a scheme has been modified in any way, then the accompanying colours should be similarly modified. All should have had the same treatment. This advice can be ignored of course, but it takes a very highly developed intuitive colour sense or a thorough understanding of the colour theories to do so successfully. There is always the danger that a strong pure colour will kill the weaker and more delicate, leaving an impression of disaster rather than the intended dynamic design.

Colour preference depends to a large extent on one's psychological make-up and few have quite the same preference. Louisa Calder is fond of selecting full strength, pure, primary and secondary colours, often in complementary relationships, and of giving precedence to one dominant colour, keeping the others subordinate. She also uses black and white as complementaries. Sometimes her strong pure colours are displayed on a partially neutralised background colour.

The proportions of spatial areas of colour in a design need to be taken into consideration, since if each area of colour is equal the result can be uninteresting. Usually a design is more successful if prominence is given to one main colour, but the main colour does not necessarily need to be presented as one large mass. It can be divided to run through the composition. Louisa Calder's banded and striped designs show how well this can work.

Designing with Crochet – Theory

As a textile, crochet lends itself to variations in both surface texture and colour, and one of these should dominate in a design; if both are present in anything like full force, the result will be an overpowering confusion devoid of any definite expression rather than the expected aesthetic creation.

If a wide range of textural variation is chosen as a theme, as when using the ornate stitch structure of traditional crochet, then the colour aspect should be played down. Indeed traditional crochet looks its best when worked in one colour only. If instead a wide range of stimulating colour play with abstract or representational colour shapes is chosen, the surface quality or grain of the fabric should take second place. This does not mean that there is no scope at all for variation in stitch, but it should remain unobtrusive, so that the surface texture does not detract from the all-important colour pattern. For this reason Louisa Calder wisely confines herself to a simple surface with only minor technical variations in stitch in order that the impact of her colours may be seen in full.

It is stating the obvious, but the overall form or shape of any article intended for functional use should suit its purpose. The cap must fit, the gloves must be long enough for the fingers. Crochet is so adaptable and easy to shape during working, and is equally easy to unravel and alter, that this should not be a problem.

Basically, Louisa Calder's designs are constructed from simple cylinders or rectangles of crochet fabric, with or without further shaping. Many modern garments are constructed on similar principles of cylindrical and rectangular shapes, and there is no reason why the ideas shown in Louisa Calder's small items should not be adapted and used on a larger scale for the making of garments such as loose tunic tops, or skirts.

It is important to keep the scale logical. A tiny article should be made up in a light-weight, fine yarn whereas a large article is better executed in a heavy-weight, thick yarn. This again is stating the obvious, but one often sees small accessory garments made up in too bulky a yarn, thus giving an impression of clumsiness which completely obliterates any design interest.

Having decided on the general theme, on the overall shape of the design, and on the yarn from which it is to be produced, the next consideration is that of decoration. Decoration can be all-over or partial, and it can be incorporated into the construction, or made up separately and applied afterwards. Decoration which is worked into the construction of any article has a very good chance of being successful as it makes use of and acknowledges a natural quality of the fabric. The technique of working crochet in straight rows or in spiral rounds results in a repetitive linear form running through the structure which can be exploited in design. Any series of repeating forms running through a design will give a suggestion of rhythm and will also give a unity which can hold a composition together. All the textile crafts are well suited to repetitive decoration because the production of these crafts is itself a repetitive hand action.

Louisa Calder's banded and striped colour patterns depend very much on interplay between the widths of each stripe, that is on the number of rows of crochet used in each. If they were all exactly matched the designs would not be so stimulating.

Decoration which is worked separately and applied afterwards allows a good deal of scope. The smaller decorative shapes can be tried out on the background and altered at will. Spatial relationships especially of the "negative" shapes in the background can then be judged in their entirety, whereas when decoration is worked as part of the construction one has to wait till the design is finished to judge the final effect. Applied decoration need not necessarily be confined to crochet motifs; any material which adds to the final effect can be employed. Louisa Calder occasionally adds "found" objects and these are not always firmly attached but are sometimes allowed mobility. There is an outlet for originality in this aspect of decoration and movement has not really been fully investigated where crochet is concerned. In one example – the interaction of metal plaques, loosely attached to her shoulder bag –

musical sound, akin to the tinkling of Chinese wind bells, results.

The subject matter of any decoration is entirely personal and expression can be unlimited. Shapes can be abstract or figurative. A designer should always attempt to analyse the imagery of any abstract patterns, repetitive or otherwise. Perhaps the shapes are suggestive of bricks, windows, footprints in the sand, birds in flight; indeed they may suggest any fanciful idea. This seemingly naïve and childlike language of forms can often lead the imagination to other related images, and the design will take over, come alive and create itself, almost as if the designer had no part in it.

Designing with Crochet – Practice

The main stitch used in Louisa Calder's designs is double crochet (American single crochet), and as it is plain and simple in appearance it must be evenly worked to look well. Uneven working tension will call attention to itself and detract from the design.

Study the chapter on Basic Techniques before starting on a design project, and work some samples of double crochet (American single crochet) in *rows*. Then for comparison, work the same stitch in *rounds*. There is a noticeable difference in the surface appearance of the two. Then work a further sample in *rows*, but pick up the back loop only of each stitch so that the work is ridged, and compare this with another sample of ridged stitches worked in *rounds*. Once again there is a difference in the surface appearance. These differences need to be taken into account if working both rounds and rows on the same article. The four textures, different yet related, can often be used to add subtle interest to a design, and in fact Louisa Calder uses them for just this purpose. They are not in themselves strong enough to detract from the colour composition.

When double crochet (American single crochet) is worked in *rounds*, the stitches do not line up one above each other absolutely vertically. There is a slight natural bias to the right. It can be shaped to a true vertical by steaming into shape with an iron barely touching the surface, or the natural bias can be accepted and even emphasised, as part of the make-up of a design.

When working in *rounds*, experiment with colour changes. Colour-based double crochet (American single crochet) patterns can be plotted on square graph paper like tapestry patterns, but it must be realised that the stitch itself is not quite a perfect square. The resultant crochet will have a more rectangular form than the graph paper plan. Any shape more complicated than a simple square or rectangle, can be more easily worked by initial planning on graph paper, for instance a pyramid shape can be planned thus:

14

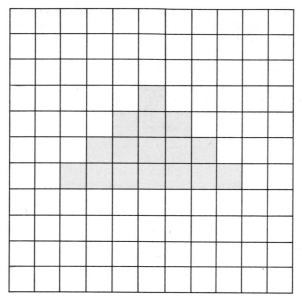

or a "window" can be expressed as:

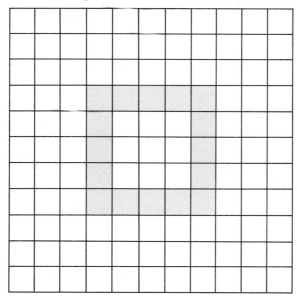

Louisa Calder's work is notable for the fascinating "spot" patterns which chase across her designs like birds in flight. They are colour changes of just one stitch at a time, or sometimes of two consecutive stitches. As explained in Basic Techniques (p. 133–5), the colours not in use are carried across the back of the work, and for the spot patterns or for any repetitive colour patterns they are carried in turn for the entire round or rounds. However, if the pattern consists of one isolated shape only, then the colour in question can be abandoned at the left-hand side of the pattern, to be picked up again on the right-hand side of the same pattern when needed for the following round.

Practice samples are also necessary to measure tension (gauge). The number of stitches per centimetre and per inch is stated for all the designs in this book where applicable. For some designs, such as the bags, neither the tension nor the resulting overall size is vitally important, although these items do need to be closely worked to give body and strength during use. Where sizing is important, with gloves for instance, stitch measurements can be altered by varying the size of the hook used. Tension depends more on the way the hook is handled during work than on the size of the hook itself. Different workers using the same yarn and same size hook will produce very varying results in measurements. If the practice sample has too few stitches to the centimetre (inch) for requirements, change to a smaller hook. If it has too many stitches to the centimetre (inch), change to a larger hook. Also, if the yarn selected for a particular area of a design should vary in thickness from the yarn used in an adjacent area, the size of the hook can be changed. For thicker yarns change to a smaller hook, and vice versa, in order to keep the width of each round or row to the required measurement. There is no reason why any design should be worked entirely on the same hook, especially when such a wide variety of yarns are involved.

Working directions are given in both metric and imperial measurements. Hook sizes and stitch names are given in both British and American forms.

Mary Konior

DRAWSTRING PURSES

Many of these purses are "fun" designs, for storing paraphernalia or for wearing on a belt. A drawstring purse is a very good article with which to make a debut in creative crochet because the shape is so simple that full attention can be given to the colours.

Each purse is worked in tubular rounds of double crochet (American single crochet) and the base is sewn up afterwards. I work in a continuous spiral but the alternative method of joining each round can be used if preferred.

Often I work the first two or three rounds at the base of each purse in ridged double crochet (American single crochet), and then continue the remainder in normal double crochet (American single crochet). There is no technical reason for beginning in this way, I just find that it adds an interesting textural variation.

Change colours every few rounds whenever the design seems to need it, which is not necessarily at the exact beginning of each round. The "steps" so produced can be used as a positive feature to aid the design. The repeating square and brick shapes give lots of scope because so many variations are possible. The spot patterns or "birds in flight" are produced by colour changes of one stitch. I change all my colours by the method given in Figure 17a of Basic Techniques (p. 134).

The purses are worked in fine, light-weight yarns, equivalent to 3 ply fingering, and they are closely worked for hard wear at a tension of 8 stitches to 2·50 cm (1"). Suggested hook size 2·50 (American sizes B/1). Full directions are given for purse A as an introductory example of the methods used.

To Work Purse A

This measures approximately 18 cm x 23 cm (7" x 9"), and requires small amounts of a main colour, with black and white, and an assortment of 8 contrasting colours.

Using the main colour leave a free end of about 75 cm (30") for sewing afterwards, and start with a foundation of 112 chain. Join into a ring with slip stitch. Work 1 double crochet (American single crochet) into each chain and continue working spirally for 4 rounds. Then work 4 rounds of contrast A, 1 round of contrast B, 4 rounds of contrast C, 4 rounds of contrast D, 4 rounds of contrast E, 2 rounds of contrast F, 4 rounds of contrast A, 1 round of contrast G, 5 rounds of contrast D, 1 round of contrast H, 17 rounds main colour

Purse A. The white squares
resemble footprints complete
with toes!

A bright and cheerful design,
easy and amusing to work.

(2 rounds of black, 2 rounds of white) twice, 2 rounds of black.

To work the "footprint" border, work (4 stitches black, 4 stitches white) repeated all the way round. Work 2 more rounds exactly the same. On the following round, alternate the colour sequence, placing white on black and black on white. Repeat this round twice more. Work 2 rounds completely in black, and 1 round in contrast D.

Drawstring purse, with stripes and chequer squares in rounds of double crochet (American single crochet).

"Steps" produced by colour
changes used as a deliberate
feature in design.

21

Change to trebles (American double crochet) and work 1 round in contrast D. Finish with 1 round of double crochet (American single crochet) in contrast H.

Sew the open base of the purse using the long end left at the beginning. I sew purses with a blanket stitch seam, but any method can be used. A double crochet (American single crochet) seam will require a longer length of yarn. Press lightly according to the requirements of the yarn. Make a drawstring chain as given in Basic Techniques (p. 137), and thread through the trebles (American double crochet), or better still, thread with leather thonging.

An idea for a dainty purse.

More purses. The repeating spot
patterns suggest "birds in flight".

23

Three purses using repeated spot
patterns, footprints and stripes
of varying widths.

24

TWO HANDBAGS

"**B**urglar's Stripes" describes the rectangular bag, which is worked in rounds and is self-explanatory, its other notable feature being the unusual asymmetrical position of the handle.

The conical bag is more complicated to work, and flutes into umbrella pleats when carried. For both designs use any tough sturdy double-knitting or sports yarn at a tension of 5 or 6 stitches to 2·50 cm (1"). Suggested hook sizes 4·00 (American sizes F/5) and 3·50 (American sizes E/4) respectively.

To Work the Conical Bag (p. 26)

A main colour and at least 3 contrast colours are needed to begin, and more can be added as work progresses. Mark the beginning of each round at first with a safety pin or coloured thread, as concentration is needed till the shaping and colour sequences can be followed by eye. Change colours as shown in Figure 17a of Basic Techniques (p. 134).

Using the main colour, start with 2 chain, work 6 double crochet (American single crochet) into the first chain next to the slip knot. Continue in spiral rounds as follows.

2nd Round: Increase by working twice into each stitch (=12 stitches).

3rd and 4th Rounds: Work without increase.

5th Round: Increase in every alternate stitch (=18 stitches).

6th Round: Keep the main colour on the left hand and pick up each contrast on the right hand as needed. Only carry the main colour at the back of the work, the contrasts can be dropped when not in use. Work 3 stitches main colour, 2 stitches contrast A, 3 stitches main, 3 stitches contrast B, 3 stitches main, 4 stitches contrast C.

7th Round: Work 5 stitches main colour, 2 stitches contrast A, 3 stitches main, 3 stitches contrast B, 3 stitches main, 4 stitches contrast C. Note that all the colour contrasts step 2 stitches to the left each time.

8th Round: Continue to work the contrasts 2 stitches to the left as before, and increase by working 2 extra stitches into each area of main colour (=24 stitches). It does not matter which main stitches are increased providing work is consistent.

9th and 10th Rounds: Work without increase, working the contrasts 2 stitches to the left as before.

11th Round: Continue to work the contrasts 2 stitches to the left, and increase by working 2 extra stitches into each area of main colour (=30 stitches). Again, it does not matter which main stitches are increased providing work is consistent.

The conical bag: see working instructions in accompanying text.

26

12th and 13th Rounds: As 9th and 10th.

Continue in this way, increasing by 6 extra stitches in every 3rd round, till the bag reaches the width required. Then work 5–8 cm (2–3") without increasing, and finish off by working 2 slip stitches. As the work grows and the contrasting spirals grow wider apart, extra spirals of colour can be added. I have added a further 3 spirals in this way. All finish in different positions, only one is carried to the top of the bag. If leather is not available for handles, work crochet handles, similar to the handle on the "Burglar's Stripes".

"Burglar's stripes", rectangular bag. Some suggestions for using stripes.

SHOULDER BAG
WITH LEATHER FACING

This shoulder bag jingles enticingly on movement and is a joy to sling on the shoulders. It has given considerable service and has been much loved and handled. The bag began as a banded pattern in rather muted harmonious shades but it then seemed to be insufficiently interesting as a

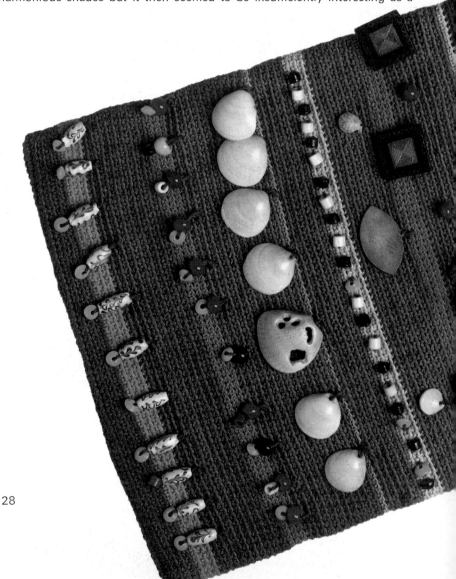

design, and I looked for some kind of decoration in order to enliven it.

Most households keep a bead or button box, and a rummage through my own hoard gave a good yield. Beachcombing is not to be despised either! Any small decorative object which can have a small hole bored through it for insertion of a sewing thread can be considered for use in this way. I have included a collection of tiny metal plaques, and have attached them to hang loosely because I considered their "flutter" to be important. The mobile pairs of beads are threaded together as shown in Figure 22b of Basic Techniques (p. 138).

This type of crochet has a natural affinity with leather, but if a suitable leather facing is unobtainable the bag can be lined and interlined with any stiff material, and thonging inserted through this. A corded chain, as shown in Figures 21a and 21b of Basic Techniques (p. 138), makes a reasonable substitute for thonging, providing that it is strongly worked with double or triple thicknesses of yarn.

The crochet fabric is closely worked in tough light-weight cotton yarns at a tension of 8 stitches to 2·50 cm (1"), suggested hook size 2·50 (American sizes B/1). The overall measurements are 24 cm x 38 cm ($9\frac{1}{2}$" x 15"), and I began at the base with 152 chain and worked in tubular rounds or ridged double crochet (American single crochet). However, there is no reason why the entire design should not be planned in a heavier yarn altogether, providing that any attachments are suitably related in scale.

THE FLAP PURSES

Purse with strong background
colour with bands.

I like to decorate both sides of these little purses in a different way. They are worked in fine yarn at a tension of 8 stitches to 2·50 cm (1"). Suggested hook size 2·50 (American sizes B/1). For a 7·50 cm (3") purse, leave an end of yarn long enough for seaming, and work 48 chain. Join into a ring with slip stitch and work rounds of double crochet (American single crochet) spirally for the depth required. Then turn and work half way back along the round. Turn again, and continue working in rows to form the flap, which can be made any size or shape by decreasing at the end of each row, or by decreasing at both the beginning and the end of each row.

31

Directions for decreasing and for making appliqué rounds and chains are given in Basic Techniques (pp. 130–1 and 139). When planning this type of design, keep the colour bands of the background crochet simple, so that the main interest is in the appliqué and its relation to the background. Work a greater assortment of appliqué motifs in different sizes and colours than will be needed, as this will allow much greater freedom and spontaneity in design. There is no reason why some of the circles should not overlap each other, or the chains intertwine, and beads or other non-crochet decoration can be added.

Sew the motifs into position before closing the base of the purse. I use a blanket stitch seam. Press lightly, being careful not to overpress the appliqué. The flap can be tucked in or fastened with a press stud.

A little crochet purse would make an unusual gift wrap for a special present.

The flaps, worked in rows, are easy to vary in shape.

Some suggestions for the free
use of appliqué.

33

34

THE NECKTIES

Not so much a play with colour, more a psychedelic romp, these dazzling ties are in tune with current ideas in fashion wear.

The ties are worked as one long spiral tube of double crochet (American single crochet) which is then flattened; I begin at one end and keep working for the whole length. In wear, the decorative pattern at one end will then "read" upside down compared with that of the other end, but this does not matter as long as the shapes look well viewed from either direction. I often prefer the ends to differ, but the orientation needs to be remembered when planning a design.

An alternative method is to work the ties in two lengths, starting at opposite extremes and meeting with a join at the back of the neck. The advantage of this method is that the shape can be more easily altered. A long length of crochet will tend to stretch in wear, and continual pulling will elongate the narrowest, weakest part, which in the case of a tie is around the back of the neck. This in turn may affect the position and size of the knot, an important consideration to the wearer. If this should happen, the fault can be easily remedied by unpicking the join at the back of the neck, unravelling some of the rounds, and rejoining.

Remember that when working rounds of double crochet (American single crochet) the stitches do not lie exactly above each other in a vertical line, but slant very slightly to the right in a natural bias. On a long necktie, this bias is too pronounced to be pressed out, and in practice it means that the colour change between stripes, which results in a "step", needs to be positioned vertically by eye and, because of the bias, this position will probably not coincide with the precise beginning of the round. Keep these "steps" on the back, or underside, of the ties, and work all decreasing and increasing on the back, in order not to detract from the main pattern on the front of the design.

Basic instructions are given for a tie measuring 7·50 cm (3") in width. Choose fine yarns, no thicker than 3 ply fingering, and work at a tension of 8

stitches to 2·50 cm (1"). Suggested hook size 2·50 (American sizes B/1). As so many different colours are required for the stripes, thicknesses may vary, and it may be necessary to use more than one size of hook in order to adjust the widths, as explained in Designing with Crochet – Practice (p. 14).

To Work the Basic Tie

Start with 48 chain and join into a ring with slip stitch. Work spiral rounds of double crochet (American single crochet) till the work measures 30 cm (12"). Then decrease 1 stitch every 1·25 cm ($\frac{1}{2}$") till there are 20 stitches left in the round. Work straight till the tie measures 68 cm (27"), or half its required length, measuring slightly stretched. As previously stated, the second half can be made separately or worked as a continuation. In the latter case, substitute increases for decreases.

When finished, press the tie lightly according to the requirements of the yarns, although the back of the neck can be more heavily pressed.

To Vary the Basic Design

The coloured stripes can be arranged in any order. I use the three primary colours plus black and white, with sometimes one or two secondary colours, and vary the sequence in which they are worked. The stripes vary between 0·60 cm ($\frac{1}{4}$") and 5 cm (2") in depth, and the deeper stripes are embellished with small repeating patterns or with larger isolated pattern units. Keep the shapes simple, relying for interest on the little echoes of colour which result from the method of changing colours.

The isolated pattern units are positioned by eye on the front of the ties and are worked all in one with the background crochet. Any simple shape that can be built up from a square component is a possibility, and shapes could be paired as mirror images.

The repeating patterns are easy to plan on the first 30 cm (12") of the tie, and merely need to be based on multiples of 6 or 8 stitches, as the total number of stitches in each round is 48. When decreasing, the repeats will need to be calculated to suit the number of stitches in the particular round being worked.

Circular or curved shapes are not so easily achieved within the basic crochet fabric as they tend to distort. I add them afterwards as appliqué rounds of ridged double crochet (American single crochet) or as appliqué chains.

To vary the texture, try introducing bands of trebles (American double crochet), both ridged and non-ridged.

A psychedelic romp – ties with
dazzling colours in simple shapes.

The pointed cap.

BONNETS, CAPS AND HATS

Concentric circular bands and stripes are the perfect decoration for head-wear because they relate to and emphasise the spherical shape of the human head. Colours can be changed according to pre-arranged deliberation, pure caprice, or because the yarn ran out!

The spot patterns which look like snow-flakes, are easier to plan if based on repeats of 8 stitches, e.g., 7 stitches main colour, 1 stitch contrast, as the total number of stitches in each round is divisible by 8.

The basic instructions can be adapted to fit any size of head, adult or child. I use different thicknesses of yarn depending on the intended wearer. The smaller designs are worked at a tension of 7 stitches to 2·50 cm (1"). Suggested hook size 3·00 (American sizes C/2 or D/3). The larger designs are worked at a tension of 6 stitches to 2·50 cm (1"). Suggested hook size 3·50 (American sizes E/4).

All are worked in spiral rounds of double crochet (American single crochet) beginning at the point. Mark the beginning of the rounds with a safety pin or coloured thread, in order to keep to an accurate shape.

THE BASIC POINTED CAP

Start with 5 chain and join into a ring with slip stitch.

1st Round: Work 8 double crochet (American single crochet) into the ring.
2nd Round: Increase by working twice into each stitch of the previous round (=16 stitches).
3rd and 4th Rounds: Work without increase.
5th Round: Increase in every alternate stitch (=24 stitches)
6th and 7th Rounds: As 3rd and 4th.
8th Round: Increase in every 3rd stitch (=32 stitches).
9th and 10th Rounds: As 3rd and 4th.
11th Round: Increase in every 4th stitch (=40 stitches).
12th and 13th Rounds: As 3rd and 4th.

14th Round: Increase in every 5th stitch (=48 stitches).

Continue in this sequence, increasing by 8 extra stitches in every 3rd round till the work measures 10 cm (4") from the beginning, then increase in every 4th round till the circumference is the required head size. Work straight without increase for 5–8 cm (2–3") or for the depth desired.

VARIATIONS ON THE BASIC POINTED CAP

The Pirate Cap

Extend the depth of the straight work. The point will then flop sideways in wear with a jaunty air, which will be all the more piratical if the design is wildly striped in scarlet. Remember to make the stripes interesting by varying their widths. The cap would be equally successful if made even longer, so that the point has a longer fall.

The Turned-back Brim

After working the basic cap, turn and work in the opposite direction for the brim. Increase 8 stitches in the next and every following 4th round till the brim is the desired depth. The brim of the hat shown is edged with a round of trebles (American double crochet) and held back with appliqué crochet circles.

The turn-back brim.

40

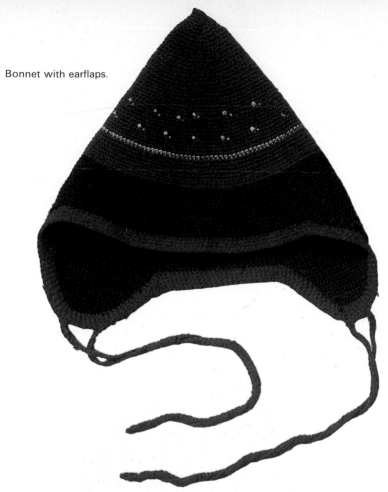

Bonnet with earflaps.

The Bonnets with Earflaps

These are enchanting on small children, and have a more exaggerated point than the basic design. Follow instructions for the Basic Pointed Cap as far as the 11th Round (40 stitches). Then increase by adding 8 extra stitches in every 4th round until the bonnet measures the required head size. Work straight for 5–8 cm (2–3").

To work the Earflaps: Starting at the beginning of the round, which is the centre back of the bonnet, work a quarter of the round plus 1·25 cm ($\frac{1}{2}$"), turn (with 1 chain) and work back for a distance of half the round plus 2·50 cm (1"). Turn again, and work in *rows* for a depth of 2·50 cm (1"), decreasing at the end of each row by omitting the last stitch. Work $\frac{1}{3}$ of the way along the next row, turn, and continue as before, decreasing 1 stitch at the end of every

41

Bonnet with earflaps
and cloche hat.

row for a further depth of 4–5 cm (1½–2"). Finish off, rejoin the yarn ⅔ of the way along the main flap and work the other ear to correspond.

To work the Edging: Using a contrasting colour, work double crochet (American single crochet) for 3 rounds, or the width preferred, around the entire edge of the bonnet. At the outer corners work 3 stitches into the same place, so that the edging lies flat.

To make the Chain Ties: Work approximately 2·50 cm (1") of chain, work double crochet (American single crochet) across the end of an earflap, work a further 2·50 cm (1") of chain, slip stitch to the beginning of the first chain thus forming a little triangle, and continue in chain for the length required. Turn, and work double crochet (American single crochet) back along the entire chain, working over the tail end of yarn as it is reached. If preferred, the tie can be reinforced with another row of work on the opposite side.

THE BASIC ROUND CAP

Start with 5 chain, join into a ring with slip stitch. 1st Round: Work 12 double crochet (American single crochet) into the ring.

The basic round cap.

43

2nd Round: Increase by working twice into every alternate stitch (=18 stitches).

3rd Round: Increase in every 3rd stitch (=24 stitches).

4th Round: Increase in every 4th stitch (=30 stitches).

5th Round: Increase in every 5th stitch (=36 stitches).

6th Round: Increase in every 6th stitch (=42 stitches).

7th Round: Increase in every 7th stitch (=48 stitches).

8th Round: Increase in every *6th* stitch (=56 stitches).

9th and 10th Rounds: Work without increase.

11th Round: Increase in every 7th stitch (=64 stitches).

12th and 13th Rounds: Work without increase.

Now follow the latter sequence, increasing 8 stitches in every 3rd round, till the work measures 7·50 cm (3") from the beginning. Then increase in every 4th round, with 8 extra stitches, till the work measures the size required.

VARIATIONS ON THE BASIC ROUND CAP

The Cloche Hats

To make a cloche, work the basic pattern to the required head size, then continue, without increasing, for a further 7·50 cm (3") or more. For the brim, increase 8 stitches in the next and every following 4th round for the depth required. To add textural interest, some parts of the design can be worked in ridged crochet.

These cloche hats are made up in sturdy sports yarns, closely worked to retain a firm shape, and decorated with appliqué crochet worked in finer yarns. Always make a larger number of crochet motifs than will actually be used for the appliqué, so that different arrangements can be tried.

I use beads and buttons for emphasis, and this idea could be developed further, and the ornamentation enriched even more.

44

The cloche hat.

THE BELTS

These belts are bright and sizzling stripes ornamented with appliqué crochet and beads. The sturdy double thickness belts are rounds of double crochet (American single crochet) pressed flat like the neckties. The single thickness belts are simple rows of double crochet (American single crochet), similar to the choker designs. The belts vary in width from 4 cm to 6 cm (1½" to 2½"), and are worked in light-weight yarns at a tension of 7 stitches to 2·50 cm (1"). Suggested hook size 3·00 (American sizes C/2 or D/3).

The white circular motif with its pronounced spiral form, is more complicated to make than the flat rounds of crochet which I usually work for appliqué, so full pattern directions are given below. The method for working the buttons is also given in detail.

The contrasting stripes on the violet coloured belt are varied by working rounds of trebles (American double crochet) between the usual double crochet (American single crochet).

Examples of double thickness
belts with suggestions for
fastening.

Chain ties, if used instead of buttons, can be worked directly on to the belt. Leave a long tail end of yarn and make a slip knot. Remove the slip knot from the hook, insert the hook into the crochet, pick up the slip knot and draw through. Now work the chain using both the main yarn and the tail end together as one thread, or work a corded chain as shown in Figure 21b of Basic Techniques (p. 138).

The Snail-shell Appliqué

Work into the back loop only of all the stitches to produce the ridge. Note that the circle does not begin in the usual way with a ring of chain. The directions are given as one continuous round.

Start with 2 chain and work 4 double crochet (American single crochet) into the first chain, next to the slip knot. Work 2 double crochet (American single crochet) into each of the next 8 stitches, 2 half trebles (American half double crochet) into each of the following 2 stitches, 2 trebles (American double crochet) into each of the following 18 stitches, 1 half treble (American half double crochet) into each of the following 4 stitches, 1 double crochet (American single crochet) into each of the following 8 stitches, 1 slip stitch into each of the following 2 stitches. Finish off, leaving an end of yarn long enough for sewing the appliqué into position.

Small Crochet Buttons

In order to keep these to a good spherical shape, stuff each button with a very hard and tightly wound little ball of the same yarn.

The directions are given as one continuous round. Start with 2 chain and work 4 double crochet (American single crochet) into the first chain next to the slip knot. Continue in double crochet (American single crochet) and work (twice into the next stitch) 10 times, then work 30 consecutive stitches. A three-dimensional shape should now have formed. Insert the stuffing and decrease by missing every alternate stitch till the gap is closed. Work 2 or 3 chain for a stem if required, and finish off leaving an end of yarn ready for sewing the button into position.

To vary the size of the button, the number of increases can be altered. To vary its appearance, the main part can be worked in ridged crochet, but in this case the decreasing should still be worked in normal crochet as otherwise it will stretch too much.

Make buttonhole loops from short lengths of chain.

Two belts showing the circular
or snail-shell motif.

47

ORNAMENTAL BUTTONS

A giant crochet button can look stunning with a corded chain as a loop fastening. Detailed designs are only really practical on a button measuring 4 cm ($1\frac{1}{2}$") or more in diameter, and for a flat, or nearly flat, button of this size, some sort of mould is necessary as a base.

Any light-weight washable substance such as wood, plastic or metal can be used as a mould. An old button is quite suitable. It is important that the mould should not be visible through the finished crochet fabric, and the latter should be worked as closely as possible for this reason. For preference, use light-weight yarns equivalent to 3 ply or 4 ply fingerings. Suggested hook size 2·50 (American sizes B/1).

To Work the Basic Button

Note that the rounds do not begin in the usual way with a ring of foundation chain. Start with 2 chain and work 6 double crochet (American single crochet) into the first chain next to the slip knot. Continue working spirally as follows.

2nd Round: Increase by working twice into each stitch (=12 stitches).
3rd Round: Increase in every alternate stitch (=18 stitches).
4th Round: Increase in every 3rd stitch (=24 stitches).

Continue in this way for the size of the mould allowing for stretch. Work 1 round without shaping, then decrease by missing a stitch in the following rounds as often as necessary to enclose the mould. Finish by gathering the back with a needle.

For a buttonhole loop, make a corded chain, as explained for drawstring chains in Basic Techniques (p. 137).

To Vary the Basic Button

Ridged and non-ridged stitches can be interchanged for textural variation. The speckles on the violet coloured button are colour changes of 2 ridged

48

stitches on a non-ridged background. The red and yellow Catherine Wheel has a colour change every 2 rounds. The black oval button is worked as a round Basic Button and then stretched to cover an oval mould. The beads are sewn into position after the rest of the work is completed.

To work the blue Snail-shell button, follow the pattern for Snail-shell appliqué, given with the Belt designs (p. 46), enlarging it if required with extra trebles (American double crochet), and finish as for the Basic Button. The red and white design begins as a Basic Button worked in ridged double crochet (American single crochet), and after 3 rounds changes to trebles (American double crochet). For these, increase in every alternate stitch of the 4th round, and in every 3rd stitch of the 5th round, and so on if necessary.

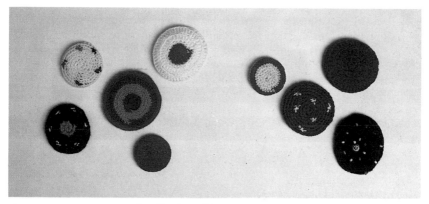

A collection of buttons including
Catherine Wheels and
Snail-shells.

GLOVES

The gloves I make are worked from wrist to finger tip in spiral rounds. The attraction of this method is that they are very easy to repair when the fingers wear out. Simply cut off the offending ragged finger, extract the loose bits of yarn, and re-work.

Choose light-weight yarns equivalent to 3 ply fingering, and work at a tension of 7 stitches to 2·50 cm (1"). Suggested hook size 3·00 (American sizes C/2 or D/3).

Basic instructions are given for an adult's right-hand glove measuring 17·80 cm (7") around the hand above the thumb, and also for a child's glove measuring 15·20 cm (6"). Each size can be varied by working to a looser or closer tension.

To Work the Basic Adult Glove

First work a test sample for assessing size. Make a foundation of 50 chain and join into a ring with slip stitch. Work 1 double crochet (American single crochet) into each chain and continue working spirally for 4 rounds. Check that there are 50 stitches. Try the sample on the hand above the thumb, and if it is too loose change to a smaller hook, if it is too tight change to a larger hook.

Start the glove with a foundation of 54 chain, and join into a ring with slip stitch. Work 1 double crochet (American single crochet) into each chain, check that there are 54 stitches, and continue working for 12·60 cm (5") or for the length required till the thumb is reached. Estimate the beginning of the round, and from now on, until the fingers are positioned, mark the beginning each time. For the thumb opening, miss the first 12 stitches of the round, and work 8 chain *loosely* instead of the missed stitches. Continue working in rounds of 50 stitches for a further 4 cm (1½") or for the length required until the base of the fingers.

For the First Finger: With the palm facing and starting at the beginning of

50 Facing page: repeating spot
patterns used to advantage.

More repeating spot patterns,
"birds in flight".

The widths of these stripes are
varied to add interest to a
simple idea.

the round, work the first 7 stitches, work 3 chain, then work the last 7 stitches of the round. Continue on these 17 stitches for 6·50 cm (2½") or for the length required. To shape the tip, * miss 1 stitch, work the next 2 stitches. Repeat from * for 2 more rounds. Finish off and draw in the opening while darning in the end.

For the Second Finger: With the palm facing, rejoin the yarn by inserting the hook into the junction of the chain and the main round at the base of the previous finger and draw the yarn through, work the next 6 stitches of the main round, work 3 chain, work the last 6 stitches of the main round, then work 3 stitches into the chain at the base of the previous finger. Work on these 18 stitches for 7 cm (2¾") or for the length required, and complete the tip as for the First Finger.

For the Third Finger: Follow directions for the Second Finger but work the length to correspond with that of the First Finger.

For the Fourth Finger: With the palm facing, work the remaining 12 stitches, then work 3 stitches into the 3 chain at the base of the previous finger. Work on these 15 stitches for 5 cm (2") or for the length required, and complete as for the other fingers.

For the Thumb: Work across the 12 stitches and into each of the 8 chain. Continue on these 20 stitches for 5 cm (2") or for the length required, and complete as for the fingers.

Work a left-hand glove to correspond, reversing the positions of the thumb and fingers. Press lightly according to the requirements of the yarn.

Thumbs in a different colour to
the other fingers add interest.

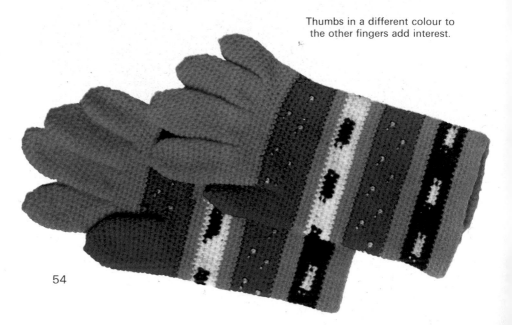

Variations of stripes and spot
patterns are endless.

To Work the Basic Child's Glove

First work a test sample for assessing size. Make a foundation of 42 chain, and join into a ring with slip stitch. Work 1 double crochet (American single crochet) into each chain and continue working spirally for 4 rounds. Check that there are 42 stitches. Try the sample on the hand above the thumb, and if it is too loose change to a smaller hook, if it is too tight change to a larger hook.

Start the glove with a foundation of 46 chain, and join into a ring with slip

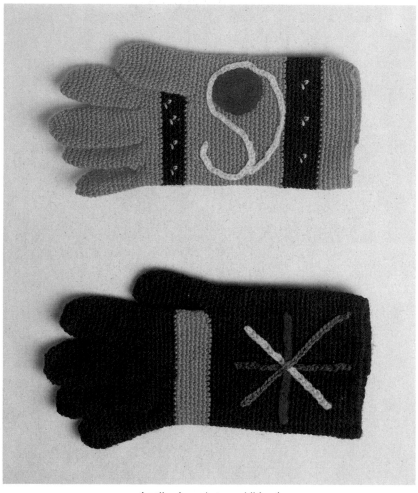

Appliqué crochet on children's gloves.

56

stitch. Work 1 double crochet (American single crochet) into each chain, check that there are 46 stitches, and continue working for 10 cm (4") or for the length required till the thumb is reached. Estimate the beginning of the round, and from now on, until the fingers are positioned, mark the beginning each time. For the thumb opening, miss the first 10 stitches of the round and work 6 chain *loosely* instead of the missed stitches. Continue working in rounds of 42 stitches for a further 3 cm (1¼") or for the length required until

More suggestions for children's
gloves.

the base of the fingers.

For the First Finger: With the palm facing and starting at the beginning of the round, work the first 6 stitches, work 3 chain, then work the last 6 stitches of the round. Continue on these 15 stitches for 4·50 cm (1¾") or for the length required. To shape the tip, * miss 1 stitch, work the next 2 stitches. Repeat from * for 2 more rounds. Finish off and draw in the opening while darning in the end.

Variations on the striped theme.

For the Second Finger: With the palm facing, rejoin the yarn by inserting the hook into the junction of the chain and the main round at the base of the previous finger and draw the yarn through, work the next 5 stitches of the main round, work 3 chain, work the last 5 stitches of the main round, then work 3 stitches into the chain at the base of the previous finger. Work on these 16 stitches for 5 cm (2") or for the length required, and complete the tip as for the First Finger.

The "step" colour change can be
placed anywhere on the palm.

For the Third Finger: Follow directions for the Second Finger but work the length to correspond with that of the First Finger.

For the Fourth Finger: With the palm facing, work the remaining 10 stitches, then work 3 stitches into the 3 chain at the base of the previous finger. Work on these 13 stitches for 4 cm (1½") or for the length required, and complete as for the other fingers.

For the Thumb: Work across the 10 stitches and into each of the 6 chain. Continue on these 16 stitches for 4 cm (1½") or for the length required, and complete as for the fingers.

Work a left-hand glove to correspond, reversing the positions of the thumb and fingers. Press lightly according to the requirements of the yarn.

Repeating spots on a child's
glove.

The "step" between colours used
to full effect.

61

To Vary the Basic Glove Designs

Colours can be changed at will to form stripes across the main part of the hand, and either of the two methods of changing colours can be used. For spot patterns use the method shown in Figure 17a of Basic Techniques (p. 134), which gives the attractive echo.

To plan repeating spot patterns on the Adult Glove: On rounds of 54 stitches, work either (7 stitches main colour, and 2 stitches contrast), or (8 main, 1 contrast), 6 times.

On rounds of 50 stitches, work either (4 main, 1 contrast), or (3 main, 2 contrast), 10 times.

To plan repeating spot patterns on the Child's Glove: On rounds of 46 stitches, work either (4 main, 1 contrast), or (3 main, 2 contrast), 9 times, with 1 extra main at the end of the round.

On rounds of 42 stitches, work either (5 main, 2 contrast), or (6 main, 1 contrast), 6 times.

DRIVING GLOVES

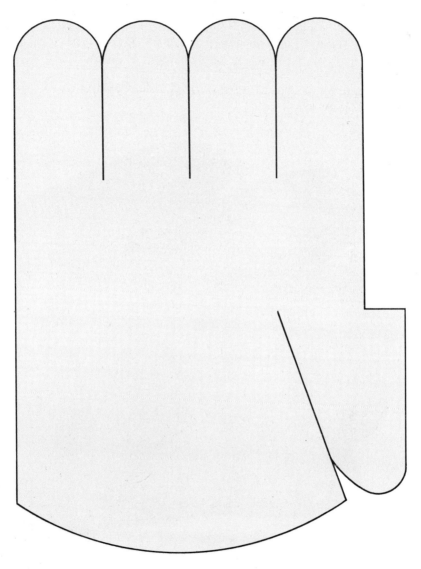

Trace pattern for the chamois
leather palm.

These are faced with chamois leather palms, as otherwise this type of glove will tend to slip on the steering wheel.

To cut the palm, first trace the outline given and cut a paper shape from which to cut the leather. The thumb folds upwards after cutting.

Position the palms temporarily on each glove with adhesive tape, in order to avoid unnecessary pin or needle marks on the leather. Overcast the edges

with a strong thread.

My driving gloves have been used and washed but they do show the position of the leather palms. If the shape needs to be larger for a large pair of gloves, cut the palms wider and re-position the slits between the fingers.

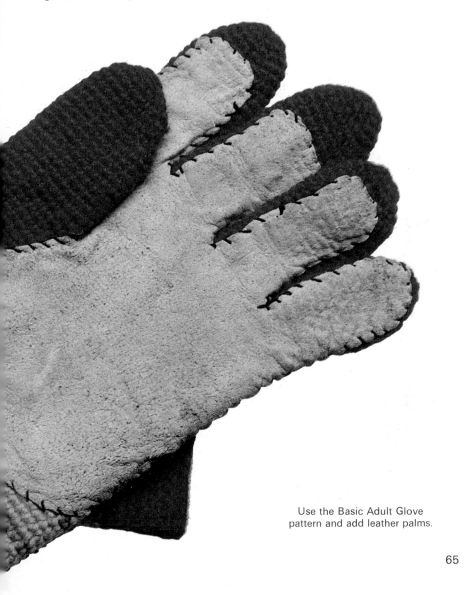

Use the Basic Adult Glove
pattern and add leather palms.

MITTENS

The repeating spot patterns which began in earlier designs as "birds in flight" are now beginning to resemble man-made missiles!

This progress, shown on the green mitten with the red brick, is because only the back loop of the contrast stitches is picked up when working the following round, and the ridge produced in this way affects the colour shape. It is worth experimenting with variations in ridged and normal, unridged, double crochet (American single crochet) when handling two colours. The methods of planning and working the repeating spot patterns are explained with the glove instructions (p. 50).

These mittens can be adapted to fit any hand, tiny, average or large, providing a test sample is worked first to assess size, in the same way as given in

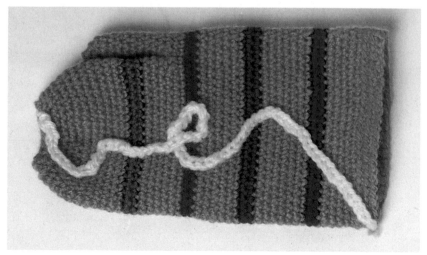

Child's mitten decorated with an
appliqué chain.

the instructions for the gloves.

Follow either of the basic glove patterns and instead of dividing for the fingers merely keep on working for the entire length of the hand. Shape the top of each mitten in the same way that the individual glove fingers are shaped.

The whole back of the hand is a good area on which to plan a design. The appliqué squiggle, with a little imagination and one eye closed, resembles a face in profile. The appliqué circle suggests a snowball balanced on a fence. Children are good at this sort of expression, so if the mittens are intended for tiny hands, let the child's own imagination contribute to the design.

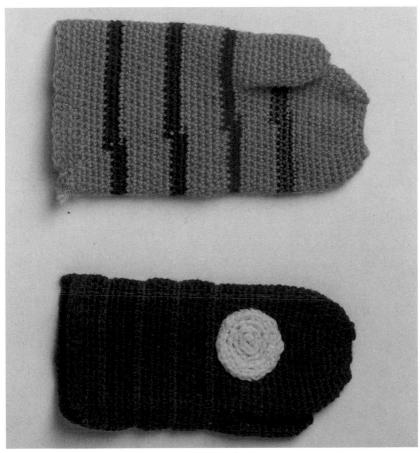

Coloured "steps" and an
appliqué "snowball".

67

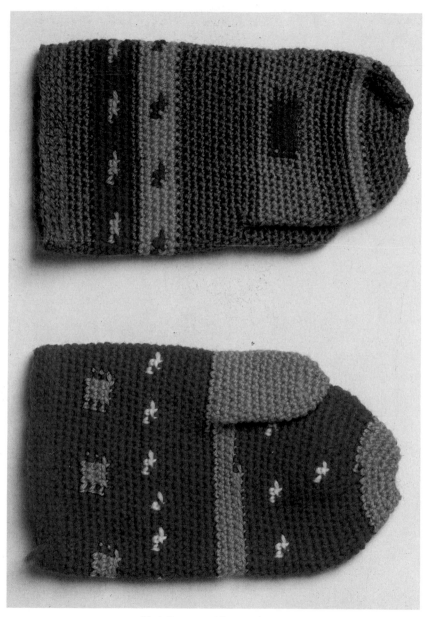

68   Variations on stripes and spot
pattern.

TEA COSIES

Bright and cheerful pot warmers are a welcome addition to the kitchen. They are intended to hang on the wall as an ornament when not in use and for this reason only one side is decorated. They are worked in spiral rounds of double crochet (American single crochet) beginning at the top.

Use a bulky yarn equivalent to two thicknesses of double-knitting or sports yarn, or use two yarns together as one, at a tension of 4 stitches to 2·50 cm (1"). Suggested hook size 5·00 (American sizes H/8).

To Work the Basic Design

Take the widest measurement around the pot measuring generously, and work a foundation chain of half this length. Join the foundation chain into a ring with slip stitch and work 2 rounds of double crochet (American single crochet).

3rd Round: Increase by working twice into every 5th stitch.

4th, 5th and 6th Rounds: Work without increase.

7th Round: Increase in every 6th stitch.

8th, 9th and 10th Rounds: Work without increase.

11th Round: Increase in every 7th stitch.

12th, 13th and 14th Rounds: Work without increase.

15th Round: Increase in every 8th stitch.

Continue in this sequence for the size required, and finish off by tapering with 2 slip stitches. Close the top either with a blanket stitch seam or with a double crochet (American single crochet) seam. In the latter case, the chain can be continued without breaking the yarn. Make a chain equal to $1\frac{1}{2}$ times the length of the seam and sew the end(s) firmly into place.

To Vary the Basic Design

Ridged crochet can be worked instead of normal crochet, and colours can be changed at will to form stripes, or repetitive colour patterns. The appliqué

69

can very well be made up in a thinner yarn than that used for the main fabric. Work a larger number of appliqué circles, in varying sizes and colours, than will actually be used in the final design so that different effects can be tried. I include round buttons to echo the circular theme. Sewing is easier to manage if it is done before the top seam is closed.

Some suggestions for appliqué
tea cosies.

SERVIETTE RINGS

If running a boarding house, or merely feeding the sort of family that gives this impression at meal times, then numbered or initialled serviette rings are a possible dining room accessory. Choose man-made, machine washable yarns, so that the rings can be washed with each change of linen if necessary.

The designs are worked in spiral rounds of double crochet (American single crochet), using light-weight yarns, at a tension of 7 stitches to 2·50 cm (1"). Suggested hook size 3·00 (American sizes C/2 or D/3).

Start with a ring of 38 chain, and work over the tail end of yarn at the beginning of the first round. Continue for a depth of 4 cm (1½"). When the last

round is completed, taper with 2 slip stitches to finish off. Darn this end in firmly as, like the appliqué, it will need to withstand the centrifugal action of a washing machine or spin dryer. Crochet the chains for appliqué as closely as possible for a neat appearance and leave the tail ends long enough for subsequent sewing. The appliqué can be pinned into position with either the back or the front of each chain facing the background fabric. Start sewing from the slip knot at the beginning of each chain, then its length can be adjusted if necessary, either by loosening the final draw through and adding extra chain, or by unpicking any excess. A complete name will be more successful if written in continuous script.

Numbered or initialled serviette
rings can be valuable table
accessories.

HAIRBANDS

All decoration is concentrated at the front of these jaunty hairbands, leaving the back quite plain.

They are worked in spiral rounds of double crochet (American single crochet) using light-weight yarns equivalent to 4 ply fingerings, at a tension of 7 stitches to 2·50 cm (1"). Suggested hook size 3·00 (American sizes C/2 or D/3).

For an average size adult hairband, make a foundation of 130 chain, join into a ring with slip stitch being careful not to allow the chain to twist, and work over the tail end of yarn at the beginning of the first round. Continue in rounds, and if the band seems too slack for the head decrease to draw the crochet in slightly as work progresses. These designs vary from 4 cm to 8 cm (1½" to 3") in depth. Taper the end of the final round by working 2 slip stitches to finish off.

74

Hairband worked in rounds of
ridged double crochet (American
single crochet).

To vary the stitch ridged crochet can be used. To make a deep band more interesting, divide the background into two colours as shown with the green and yellow design. Then blur or soften the dividing line by adding appliqué crochet, buttons, or beads.

The repeating dashes on the green-yellow band, and the triangle on the turquoise band, are worked in one with the crochet fabric, changing colours as shown in Figure 17a of Basic Techniques (p. 134). The circular motifs, beads and buttons are sewn on afterwards. Make more circular motifs in assorted colours and sizes than will actually be used, in order to try out ideas. There is no reason why the appliqué motifs should not overlap or be lavishly superimposed on each other.

More ideas for hairbands with appliqué crochet, beads and buttons.

75

CHOKERS AND HEAD RIBBONS

C rochet ribbons will brighten a dull day, a dull outfit or a dull mood. They are very quick and easy to make and are self-explanatory. Both neck and head ribbons are emphasised in some way at their centres, but otherwise the designs are not necessarily symmetrical. Part of their charm is due to the mobility of the hanging beads.

76

Head ribbon with appliqué and
beads.

More ideas for head ribbons.

Make sure the yarns chosen are washable. White especially will need to be
kept in pristine condition. I use light-weight yarns at a tension of 8 stitches to
2·50 cm (1″), and work in rows of 10 or 12 double crochet (American single
crochet). Suggested hook size 2·50 (American sizes B/1).

Details for working and attaching the appliqué are given in the chapter on

Basic Techniques (p. 139). The chokers are finished with a pair of chain ties at each end. The pairs can be worked as one by making a length of chain, then slip stitching across the end of the choker, working 1 slip stitch into each double crochet (American single crochet), and continuing with a matching length of chain. The tail end of yarn at the beginning of the chain can be hooked through with the working yarn as the chain is made to save darning in.

Press lightly before attaching the beads. Long ribbons of double crochet (American single crochet) will always tend to curl at the ends, even if heavily overpressed.

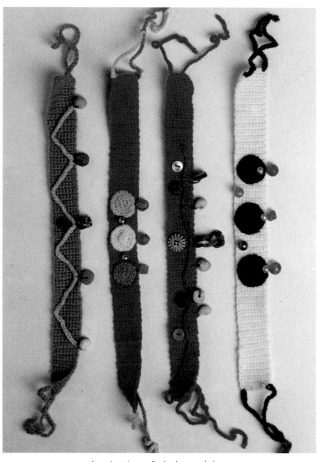

A selection of chokers giving
ideas for bead decoration.

BRACELETS

These bracelets cling closely to the arm while stretching enough to slip over the hand. They are designed to be worn just above the wrist, but there is no reason why a larger size should not be worn above the elbow on a bare arm.

The bracelets are worked in spiral rounds of double crochet (American single crochet) using light-weight yarns equivalent to 4 ply fingering, at a tension of 7 stitches to 2·50 cm (1″). Suggested hook size 3·00 (American sizes C/2 or D/3). Because of the clinging fit, choose fairly smooth yarns which will not itch or irritate in wear.

Quick-to-make bracelets in
rounds of double crochet
(American single crochet).

79

For an adult sized bracelet, start with a ring of 54 chain, and work over the tail end of yarn at the beginning of the first round. Continue in rounds, changing colours at whim, for a depth of 6·50 cm (2½″), and taper the end of the final round by working 2 slip stitches before finishing off. Darn in the end very securely as the bracelet will have to withstand a great deal of pulling and tugging.

The small repeating patterns dashed across the copper coloured bracelet consist of (4 stitches contrast, 5 stitches main colour) repeated all the way round, for 2 rounds.

The white panel on the turquoise bracelet is actually worked as a square. The natural bias of double crochet (American single crochet) worked in rounds gives it a totter to the right.

The circular motifs and beads are sewn on afterwards. The beads which are attached to the outer edge of the striped bracelet, and which are most attractive in wear, should be sewn to the final round for strength and not to the opposite weaker edge of the foundation chain.

Further ideas for bracelets.

CUSHION COVERS

These cushions are intended to inspire an easy-going light-hearted approach to creative design. Aim at producing a play cushion fit to throw around the room, rather than a treasured object to be revered. Originality is more easily achieved with this attitude, seriousness can come later with experience.

The designs are worked in rounds, seaming top and bottom afterwards. Use double knitting or sports yarn. Suggested hook size 4·50 (American sizes G/6). Tension is not of absolute importance but needs to be tested in order to calculate the number of stitches required, as usually the cover has to be fitted to the cushion rather than vice versa.

One of the practical problems in designing a large article is to estimate in advance the total quantities of yarn required. As a very rough guide, allow approximately 325 gm (10 oz) double knitting for a 36 cm (14") square cushion, depending on the type of yarn, whether pure wool or man-made, and on how loosely or tightly it is spun. If one colour runs out, take on another and let chance influence the design. Providing that a change of colour is a success in the context of the whole design it does not matter whether its presence is deliberate or whether it was a necessity to eke out a main colour.

The circular motifs are added afterwards as appliqué. All other patterns are worked into the crochet fabric. The red sun on the "blue sky" cushion is an enlargement of the Snail-shell pattern given with the belt designs (p. 46). Thinner yarns (with a smaller hook) can be used for the appliqué if preferred, and it is a good idea to work a greater assortment of circles than will actually be used in the final design to allow more freedom of experiment.

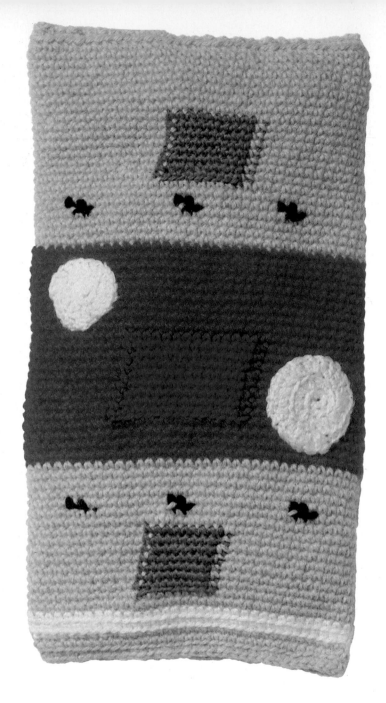

Play cushions worked in rounds
of double crochet (American
single crochet).

84 Cushions decorated with rounds
of crochet appliqué.

SLIP-ON CASES AND COVERS

Any article needing protection, such as spectacles or a treasured make-up compact, can be easily provided with a slip-on cover. Work tubular rounds of double crochet (American single crochet) for the size and shape required and seam the open base afterwards.

The yarn and hook size should be chosen in relation to the size of the intended casing. A tiny case really does need to be worked in a fine yarn with a small hook in order to keep to an appropriate scale.

Coloured decoration can be worked in with the rounds as these stripes and

86   Slip-on cases. The yellow case
is worked in ridged double
crochet (American single
crochet).

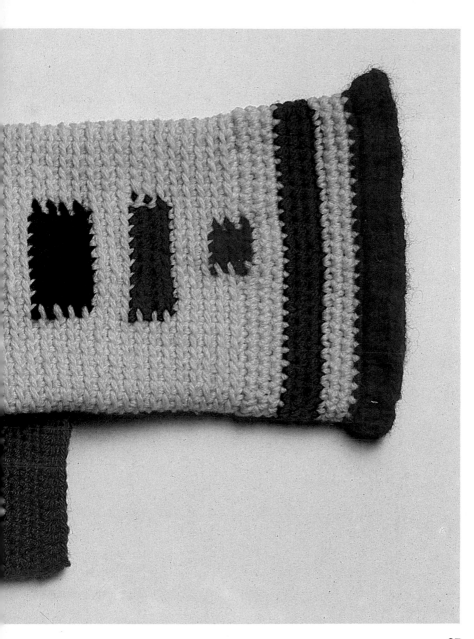

rectangles are, or appliqué circles and other decoration can be added after-wards but before seaming the base.

The decoration is worked by my usual method of changing colours as shown in Figure 17a of Basic Techniques (p. 134). The black rectangle which is displayed so very clearly on the yellow case gives a false impression of being sewn into place afterwards, but in fact it is worked in one with the background fabric, and the apparent "sewing" is the natural result of working *ridged* double crochet (American single crochet) while changing colours.

The fluted edge consists of 2 trebles (American double crochet) worked into each stitch of the previous round. Taper the finish of the edging by work-ing 1 half treble (American half double crochet), 1 double crochet (American single crochet) and 2 slip stitches before breaking the yarn.

For extra protection, the finished case can be lined with a suitable fabric. Fold the lining fabric at the base and cut to the shape of the crochet allowing for seams at top and sides. Sew the side seams, insert the lining into the case, and turn in the top edge of the lining. Sew neatly into position with a single ply of the crochet yarn if it is strong enough. A stiffened interlining can be inserted between the lining and the crochet if an especially firm casing is needed.

Alexander Calder's spectacle
case. An experiment with
embroidered initials.

Alexander Calder's Spectacle Case

This well worn example is included in order to encourage experimentation. A step away from the obvious and easy can release all sorts of unexpected creative ideas.

The main crochet fabric could have been more easily produced if worked in rows lengthways as one long strip, folded in two and seamed at the sides, but I wanted to see what would happen if I worked the fabric in rounds running lengthways and then cut it to open out as a strip.

Having cut the fabric I then lined the entire strip with black linen, turning the lining over the raw cut edges to bind them. This method is only likely to be successful with very closely worked double crochet (American single crochet), as trebles (American double crochet) or any other of the basic crochet stitches, given half a chance, will shred badly on cutting.

I then embroidered the strip, folded the work in two, and seamed the sides leaving 4 cm (1½") unseamed at the top for ease of access. The initials and leaf motif are embroidered in single feather stitch, and the dots, which at a quick glance could be mistaken for French Knots, are actually short lengths of thick yarn pulled through the background crochet and clipped to form tufts. Herringbone and interlaced blanket stitch complete the seams.

PIN CUSHIONS

Salvaged tea leaves and coffee grounds are a fair modern equivalent of the bran which was traditionally used to stuff pin cushions. Squeeze out used tea or coffee bags and spread the contents to dry in an airing cupboard. Make an inner cotton lining for the pin cushion and pack down the stuffing firmly.

These pin cushions are closely worked using fine yarns equivalent to 3 ply fingering, at a tension of 8 stitches to 2·50 cm (1"). Suggested hook size 2·50 (American sizes B/1). They are worked in rounds of double crochet (American single crochet) which are afterwards sewn up at the top and bottom to enclose the inner cushion.

For an 8 cm (3") cushion, leave an end long enough for seaming, and make 48 chain. Join into a ring with slip stitch and work spirally for a depth of 8 cm (3"). Taper the end of the last round with 2 slip stitches to finish off, leaving another end of yarn long enough for seaming.

The pyramid and flag decorations are an integral part of the crochet fabric and can be planned on graph paper if preferred. The appliqué circles and chains are added before the seams are closed.

Any bead decoration need not necessarily be sewn into place. The traditional way was to fix the beads into position with large headed pins, and this still seems a logical method, in keeping with the purpose of a pin cushion. A firm, hard stuffing is essential to hold beads in this way.

Miniature pin cushions in fine
yarns.

SLIPPER SOCKS

These cheerful, slightly zany socks have been a great success. The left and right foot are each worked alike and can be made to fit any size.

The main part of the foot is worked in spiral rounds beginning at the toe, and then the heel is worked in rows. The tension is 8 stitches to 2·50 cm (1″), working in a yarn equivalent to 3 ply fingering, but the socks could equally well be worked in a thicker yarn at 7 or even 6 stitches to 2·50 cm (1″). Suggested hook sizes 2·50, 3·00 and 3·50 respectively (American sizes B/1, C/2 or D/3, and E/4 respectively).

To Work the Basic Sock

Measure around the width of the foot (about half way along its length) and work a foundation chain of half this measurement. Join into a ring with slip stitch. Work 1 round of double crochet (American single crochet), then continue working spirally but increase by working twice into every 8th stitch till the work is wide enough for the foot. Continue without further increase till the work measures half the total length of the foot, with the crochet slightly stretched.

To work the Under-heel: Estimate the beginning of the round and mark it. Work for a distance of $\frac{1}{3}$ of the next round, turn (with 1 chain) and work back to the beginning of the round, then turn again and work in rows on these stitches till the sock when slightly stretched measures the total length of the foot. Work 5 more rows, decreasing by omitting two stitches at the end of each of these rows.

To work the Back-heel and Sides: Do not break the yarn but turn the work sideways and work into the side edge of the under-heel till the main part of the foot is reached. Slip stitch to the nearest stitch on the main foot, turn, and work back along the same side edge, continue round the curve at the back of the heel and down the opposite side edge. Slip stitch similarly to the nearest stitch on the main foot, turn, and continue to work in rows in this way.

Comfortable and cheerful slipper
socks can be made to fit any
size.

93

The small child's slipper sock
with a simpler heel shaping.

94

There is no need to work the usual 1 chain to turn the rows, as the slip stitch takes the place of the turning chain. After working about 2·50 cm (1″) in depth, try the sock on the foot to see if the sides cling sufficiently to the heel. If they do not, decrease in several places, as shown in Figure 13a of Basic Techniques (p. 131), to pull in the sides for a more snug fit, while working the remaining rows to the depth desired.

To work the Front Tongue: This is optional but is useful as a hold for pulling on the sock. Do not break the yarn at the last slip stitch, but continue across the main front of the sock. Work in rows, decreasing at both ends of every row as shown in Figure 13a of Basic Techniques (p. 131), and this will give a nice smooth shape to the edge.

Finally, sew the toe seam.

To Vary the Basic Sock

The main part of the sock, where the rounds are worked without shaping, is the obvious area on which to plan colour changes for stripes or for the smaller repeating patterns. If, depending on the total number of stitches to a round, the repeating colour changes do not work out to be mathematically correct, hide any discrepancies under the sole of the foot. Any appliqué is easier to attach if sewn into position before the toe seam is closed.

To Work the Small Child's Slipper Sock

Because of its small size, this has a simpler heel shaping. Work as for the Basic Sock, in rounds, for half the length of the foot, then turn (with 1 chain) and work back for a distance of half the round, turn again, and work in rows on these stitches till the sock when slightly stretched measures the total length of the foot.

To work the Back-heel: Make a chain equal to half the length of the previous row, and join the chain to the opposite end of the same row to form a circle. Work one round, then decrease by missing every 3rd stitch of each round, finishing at the centre of the circle.

Work the front tongue if required as for the Basic Sock.

BABY BOOTEES

Babies respond well to strong colours, and many mothers will welcome a departure from the pastel tints of traditional baby-wear.

The main ankle area can be divided into coloured bands, or the soles can be worked in a contrasting colour. The bootees also look well with an appliqué crochet chain added afterwards as a welt. If drawstring or tie chains are used at the ankle, attach them firmly just at the back of each bootee.

The basic design measures 9 cm ($3\frac{1}{2}$″) in foot length and is worked in light-weight yarn at a tension of 7 stitches to 2·50 cm (1″). Suggested hook size 3·00 (American sizes C/2 or D/3). The left and right foot are each worked alike, and the bootees can be adapted for larger or smaller feet by varying the hook size and thus varying the tension.

To Work the Basic Bootee

Start at the ankle with 42 chain and join into a ring with slip stitch. Work spiral rounds of double crochet (American single crochet) for 4–5 cm ($1\frac{1}{2}$–2″). Turn (with 1 chain) and work 28 stitches, turn again, and work in rows on these stitches for the front foot, decreasing 1 stitch at the end of every row till 8 stitches remain. Break off yarn.

To work the heel, insert the hook at the right-hand side of the 14 stitches left on the main round, draw the yarn through, and work in rows across these stitches, increasing 1 stitch at the beginning and end of the next and every following row till there are 22 stitches. Before turning each row, slip stitch to join to the corresponding row on the front foot, and omit the turning chain.

Now work in rounds, along the side of the front foot, across the toe, along the other side and across the back heel. Work 4 rounds altogether, ending at the centre back heel. Work the next 3 stitches, turn (with 1 chain) and work back 6 stitches, turn again and work the sole in rows, increasing 1 stitch at the end of every row till there are 14 stitches. Work without increasing till the sole measures 7·50 cm (3″) altogether. Decrease 1 stitch at both ends of every row till 6 stitches remain. Finish off. Turn the bootees inside out and sew the sole into position.

Baby bootees with a modern
look.

PRAM OR COT COVERS

Coloured panels are a good way of breaking up a large rectangular area to make the design more decorative. A very large cover or blanket which could be unwieldy to work because of its size, can also be more easily handled if worked in separate panels which are afterwards joined.

As a very rough guide allow approximately 325 gm (10 oz) double-knitting or sports weight yarn for a pram cover measuring 46 cm x 61 cm (18" x 24"), depending on the type of yarn, whether pure wool or man-made, and on how loosely or tightly it is spun. Tension is not of great importance; the suggested hook size 4·50 (American sizes G/6). These covers are worked in rows running either widthways or lengthways. The green-violet counterchange design is worked as two separate panels, as is the small green-yellow design. The latter was intended originally as a place mat for a table setting, but it is included here as the method is similar, with a panel of ridged double crochet (American single crochet) joined to a panel of ridged trebles (American double crochet). The remaining designs are worked all in one piece with colour changes forming the decorative panels, although these too could be worked separately if an especially large cover is planned. The multicoloured panel design is worked widthways in normal double crochet (American single crochet), the white-violet cover is worked lengthways in ridged crochet.

Ridged crochet is worked by inserting the hook under only one loop of the stitch beneath, as explained in Basic Techniques (p. 133), and either the front loop or the back loop can be used providing the work is consistent. When working *rounds* the back loop is the only logical choice, as this leaves the front loop "unused" on the front of the work, and traditionally people continued to use the back loop when working in *rows*. However, I work on the front loop, and the resultant rows lie flat and expand in height. If the back loop is used instead, the rows corrugate and contract in height. This effect is especially noticeable when working double crochet (American single crochet) but is not quite so pronounced with trebles (American double crochet). The two

Green-violet counterchange
design, worked as two separate
panels.

99

methods of ridging are worth comparing, and both could be used in different panels on the same design.

For the appliqué circles, use rounds of ridged double crochet (American single crochet) as well as the larger Snail-shell appliqué given with the Belt designs (p. 46). Use thinner yarns with a smaller hook for the appliqué to avoid a look of clumsiness for the smaller shapes.

The appliqué braid covering the seam on the green-violet counterchange design consists of two rows of double crochet (American single crochet) worked lengthways.

The frilled edging consists of 4 trebles (American double crochet) worked into every stitch of the row beneath, again using a thinner yarn and smaller hook.

Press the finished cover lightly, depending on the type of yarn, being careful not to overpress the appliqué.

100

Two covers with stripes and circles used as elements of design.

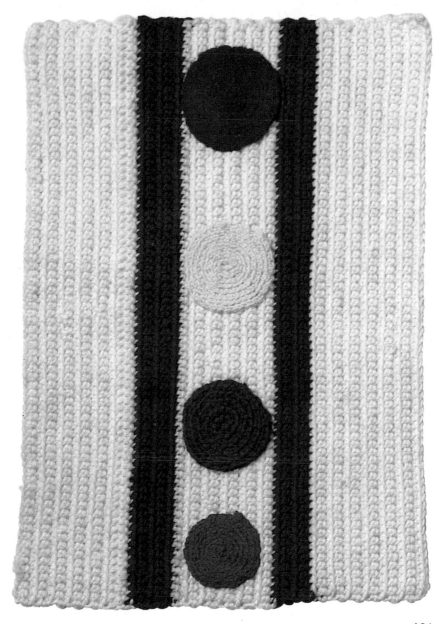

TABLE MATS

L ay an inviting table with mats designed especially for a set of favourite china. Choose heavy yarns to complement pottery, or fine yarns to complement delicate china. The circular mats are worked in ridged double crochet (American single crochet) and in ridged trebles (American double crochet), and both types can be enlarged to any size. Yarns should be machine washable and cotton would be a good choice. The mats shown are worked in light-weight yarns at a tension of 7 stitches to 2·50 cm (1"). Suggested hook size 3·00 (American sizes C/2 or D/3).

In order to keep large circles of crochet absolutely flat, care is needed in counting the increases, otherwise the outer edges may tend either to frill or to pull inwards.

To Work the Double Crochet Mat (American Single Crochet)
Start with 5 chain, join into a ring with slip stitch.
1st Round: Work 8 double crochet (American single crochet) into the ring and continue working spirally in ridged double crochet (American single crochet) marking the beginning of each round.
2nd Round: Increase by working twice into every stitch.
3rd Round: Increase in every alternate stitch (=24 stitches).
4th Round: Work without increase.
5th Round: Increase in every alternate stitch (=36 stitches).
6th Round: As 4th.
7th Round: Increase in every 3rd stitch (=48 stitches).
8th Round: As 4th.
9th Round: Increase in every 4th stitch (=60 stitches).

Continue in this way, adding 12 extra stitches on alternate rounds, till the work reaches the required size, ending on a round without increases. As an edging, work 1 round of trebles (American double crochet), with increases, tapering the end of this round by working 1 half treble (American half double

Opposite page – These mats can
be executed in a variety of sizes.

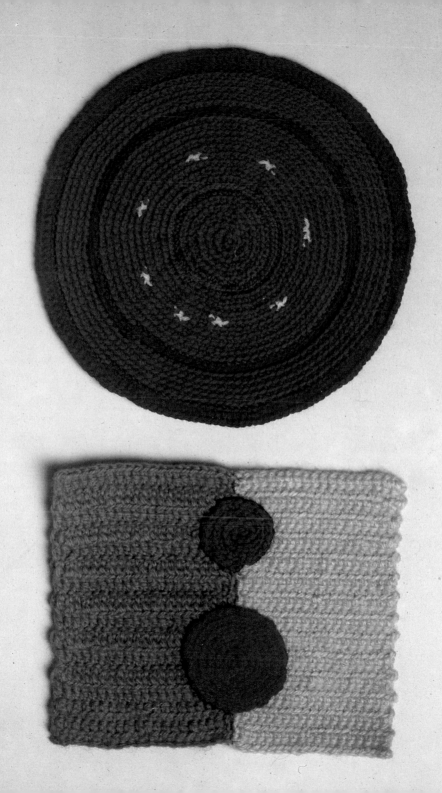

crochet), 1 double crochet (American single crochet), 2 slip stitches, before finishing off. Press lightly according to the requirements of the yarn.

To Vary the Basic Design

Concentric rings of colour can be introduced by working 1 or 2 rounds in a contrast, or repeating patterns can be planned in multiples of 2, 4, 6 or 12 stitches, as the number of stitches in each round is divisible by 12. The red repeats splashed on the yellow mats are squares, 2 stitches wide and 2 rounds deep. The blue streaks are rectangles, 6 stitches wide and 2 rounds deep. The "breadcrumbs" on the violet mat consist of 2 stitches in white.

To vary the working method, each round can be joined separately instead of being worked as a continuous spiral.

To vary the design, plain stitches can be used instead of the ridged stitches, or the main stitch can be changed to trebles, as shown in the small mats. If using the latter, the increases need to be adjusted as follows:

To Work the Treble Mat (American double crochet)

Work the first 2 rounds of the Double Crochet Mat (American single crochet), then change to trebles (American double crochet).

3rd Round: Increase by working 2 trebles (American double crochet) into every alternate stitch (= 24 stitches).

4th Round: As 3rd (= 36 stitches).

5th Round: Increase in every 3rd stitch (= 48 stitches).

6th Round: Increase in every 4th stitch (= 60 stitches).

7th Round: Increase in every 5th stitch (= 72 stitches).

Continue to enlarge the mat as required, adding 12 extra stitches in every round. For the edging work 1 round of double crochet (American single crochet) without increases, tapering with 2 slip stitches to finish off.

Opposite page – Three round table mats.

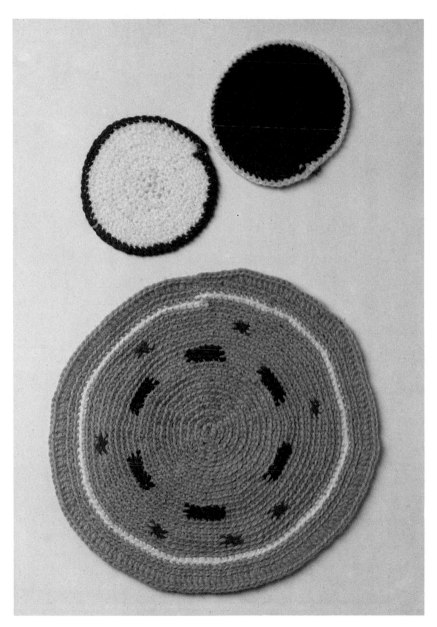

RUGS AND WALL HANGINGS

The sumptuous pile of a hooked rug is always a delight to run one's fingers through, and there is no need to be afraid of embarking on what seems to many to be a marathon effort, for although a certain amount of dogged endurance is required, a rug can be worked at odd moments and is a wonderfully relaxing occupation.

The initial enthusiasm of starting a hooked rug is more likely to be sustained to the finish if the design is a personal creation too. Sometimes I have used designs of my granddaughter, Andrea, sometimes those of my husband, but usually I have used my own ideas.

Forget the typical rug kit designs and try a fanciful approach to imaginative textile painting. Try spiky grasses, falling leaves and forms of plant growth; try whirling spirals and similar symbols of flying and pursuit; try multicoloured discs, balloons or planets in orbit; try whimsical insects or animals; try any idea that has never been worked as a rug before.

Planning can be done directly on the canvas, or a small drawing can be squared up and enlarged to fit the canvas. Many rug canvases have a square grid of coloured threads at 7·50 cm (3") intervals which are useful for enlarging a small drawing.

Materials and Preparation for Hooked Rug Making

Hooked rugs are usually worked in bulky 6 ply rug yarns on cotton canvas with a mesh of 10 holes to 7·50 cm (3"). The pile can be worked with a normal crochet hook, but a latch hook, especially designed to a standard size suitable for the mesh, enables a much more efficient action. A gauge is needed for cutting the yarn into short pieces approximately 7·50 cm (3") in length.

Some manufacturers supply yarns ready-cut and packaged into bundles, but hanks are required as well because longer lengths of yarn are needed for binding the edges of the finished rug. Acrylic yarns are now available, and the

106

Try any idea that has never been
worked as a rug before.

resultant rugs are easier to wash than the traditional pure wool rugs. Thinner carpet yarns, often obtainable from carpet factories, can also be used with a latch hook, in which case, use two or three thicknesses to increase bulk.

To prepare the canvas, turn the raw cut edges forward to the front of the work, allowing turnings of 2·50–4·00 cm (1–1½″) so that the meshes exactly coincide. (The pile is then worked over the double thickness of canvas, omitting the extreme outer edge which is bound afterwards).

Outline the design with waterproof marking ink using a paint brush. Once the design has been outlined and the colours planned, the total amounts of yarn required can be calculated by counting the number of holes to each area, which will give the number of pieces needed in each colour. Quantities are easy to calculate if ready-cut bundles are used, as the number of pieces is usually stated on the pack. If using hanks, cut an entire hank first, and either count the pieces or work some of the canvas to assess the area covered by one hank.

Whimsical insects.

Spinning and whirling shapes.

110

Andrea's rug.

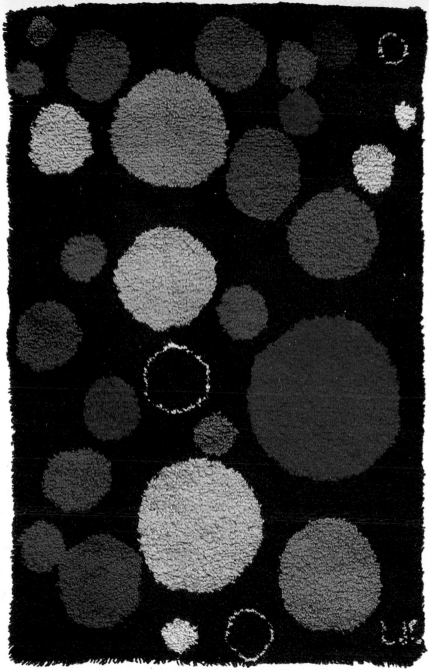

Multicoloured balloons.

Primary colours used to make an
abstract design.

To Work the Pile

Fold a cut piece of yarn around the shaft of the hook, then insert the hook under the double weft thread so that the latch is open (Figure 1a). Place the 2 cut ends inside the hook (Figure 1b). Draw the hook back so that the latch closes and the cut ends are pulled back through the loop originally folded around the shaft. Tighten the knot afterwards (Figure 1c). Work all knots in the same direction so that the pile lies one way.

To Finish the Rug

Reinforce the selvedges and folded edges with a plaited binding. Using a very large-eyed needle, and working from left to right, work a figure-of-eight stitch, 3 holes forward (Figure 2a) and 2 holes back (Figure 2b). Rugs should not be lined as this would trap grit and dirt.

Spiky grasses in a landscape.

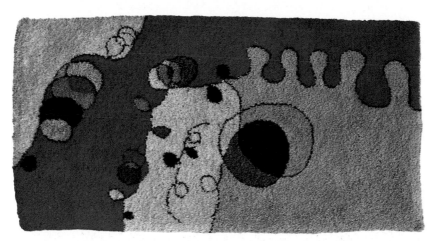

Top – Abstract design.
Bottom – Mythical animals.

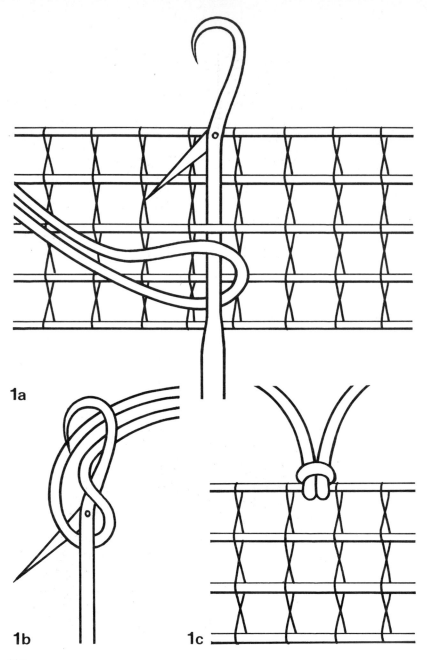

1a

1b

1c

116

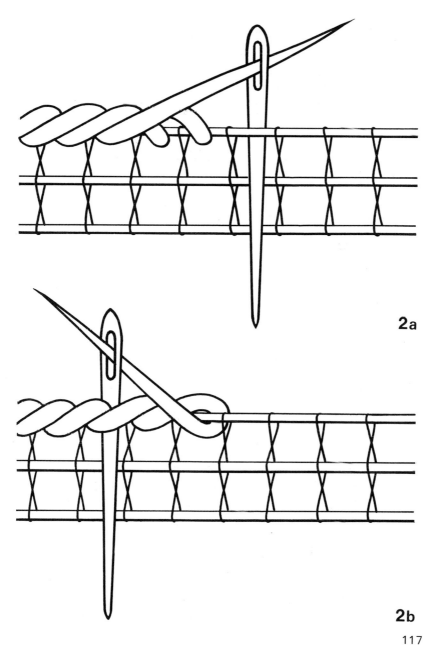

2a

2b

MATERIALS AND EQUIPMENT

A range of hooks in different sizes and an assortment of yarns are the basic materials needed for crochet, backed up by the usual work-box aids of scissors, tape measure, crewel or darning needles, dressmaker pins and safety pins.

Hooks

These are manufactured in a variety of substances including steel, aluminium, plastic, casein, wood and bone, the finest sizes (for traditional lace crochet) being made of steel, and the largest giant sizes (for bulky yarns) being made of casein or wood. The intermediate "wool" sizes are usually made of a light-weight coated metal such as aluminium.

A good serviceable hook should be smooth with a well defined pointed head designed to be pushed easily through the fabric, and with a well defined notch to catch the yarn. The thickness of the shaft determines the size, for this determines the size of the stitch produced. The size of the head is of secondary importance; in fact, if hooks of the same size but of different manufacture are compared they will be found to have completely different heads.

Manufacturers are gradually changing to the International Standard Range of hook sizes which was introduced in 1969. This new range of metric sizes refers to the cross-section diameter of the hook measured in millimetres. It is now in general use in Britain and Europe, in the Commonwealth countries, and in many other parts of the world, with the notable exceptions of America and Japan. The table gives a comparison of the International Standard Range with the current American Ranges.

The precise size of the hook is not as important as the manner in which it is handled and the resulting tension or gauge of the fabric produced. The variation in tension of crochet produced by different workers is considerable, and often the hook size recommended by a pattern needs to be changed in order to work to the required tension and overall dimensions. A good average size useful for learning to crochet is an ISR 3·50 or 4·00 (American sizes E/4 or F/5), which is suitable for medium-weight yarns or for double-knitting or sports yarns.

Comparison of Hook Sizes
The following table is a guide only, since the sizes do not exactly correspond.

American	International Standard Range
B/1	2·50
C/2	3·00
D/3	
E/4	3·50
F/5	4·00
G/6	4·50
H/8	5·00
I/9	5·50
J/10	6·00
K/10$\frac{1}{2}$	7·00

Yarns
A wide variety of yarns advertised for hand knitting and crochet is available in different fibres, plies, and colours, and with different spins. Knitting yarns with brand names belong to the world of fashion and do not always stay long on the market. They usually carry bands or labels giving a statement of composition and other information including vat number and dye lot, which identifies a particular batch of yarn in manufacture. When making a fashion garment it is essential to check that matching colours carry the same mark, although this is not a problem when selecting yarns for creative work. For these designs, the wider assortment of dyes available, the better, and it is not expected that such yarns would be bought en masse. Quite small amounts are useful, and a good collection can be built up from yarns left over from other work. It may be necessary to buy a main colour, but once it becomes known that yarns are gratefully received, odd donations will roll into the family wool bag.

Most yarns are plied, that is they are composed of separate strands which are then twisted together. Those with a tight or high twist, such as crepe yarns, are very good for crochet work because a high twist is less likely to be split by the hook during work. It is all too easy with a lesser twist, to split the yarn accidentally and then to have to work the spoilt split stitch again.

A ply is not a standard thickness of strand. At one time the terms two ply three ply and four ply fingerings were used to describe wools of recognisable weights or thicknesses, but present-day variations in ply are utterly confusing. Some spinners use two plies always, but these can be two thin plies, two thick plies, or two intermediate plies. Other spinners base their yarns on one thin basic ply, and making it up into yarns of two, three or four plies. The one thin basic ply also differs among spinners, so that a three ply by one manufacturer can equal the four ply of another. The range is further increased by the quick-knit, double and bulky yarns now on the market, which are usually loosely spun in a thick basic ply, and again the component ply of these yarns can vary considerably. The double-knitting or sports yarns are especially

1

popular and widely used for outdoor garments. They are also an excellent choice for a beginner learning to crochet, being neither too bulky nor too fine for the purpose, and stitches are easily distinguished.

Breaks in yarns can be invisibly mended by splicing. Sometimes a "rogue" ball will have several manufacturer's knots, and it is an improvement technically if these are taken out and the ends rejoined by splicing. To splice two ends of yarn together, separate the plies, no matter how many strands there are, and graduate the lengths of the separated strands. Overlap the two ends (Figure 1), and rub the overlap till the fibres cling, using the palms of the hands, slightly moistened. The total overlap needs to be of sufficient length to thread on the hand in crochet, say approximately 25 cm (10"). Pure wools usually splice more successfully than man-made yarns, but even a splice that does not seem to cling very successfully in itself should be unnoticeable in the finished crochet. *Figure 1, How to splice yarns.*

When searching for yarns, it may be worth looking for sources other than the obvious. Any yarn strong enough to withstand the pull of a hook can be regarded as suitable for crochet. Weaving, tapestry, or carpet yarns may be useful. There is no such thing as a good or a bad yarn in itself, but a particular yarn chosen should be suitable for the purpose of the article being made. It is logical to reserve the softest, most delicate yarns for purposes of cosseting,

120

such as protection of the baby or of one's own skin. Loosely spun but coarser yarns are suitable for purposes of insulation rather than hard wear – and coarse yarns with a high twist are suitable for articles requiring hard wear.

Any subsequent requirements of hygiene such as dry cleaning and laundering should be taken into account, and synthetic and natural fibres kept apart as far as possible, as each ideally needs a different treatment. The ideal is not always attainable as often the individual yarns themselves are a blend of man-made and natural materials. It may be advisable to test wash a yarn of unknown age or composition to see whether it is dye-fast or whether it will shrink or stretch.

These designs often require very short lengths of a particular colour and these can sometimes be acquired by devious means. A short length can be un-ravelled from the weft of a woven fabric such as a wool tweed. Or a thin yarn can be obtained by dividing the ply of a thicker yarn.

Extreme creativity could follow the Back-to-the-Earth movement and include the initial spinning. Hedgerows can be combed in sheep-farming areas for adhering fleece, from which hand-spun yarn can be made. It is not comparable to manufactured yarn, and a lumpy unevenness is considered to add to the charm of hand-spun wool. Small amounts are suitable for working a single contrasting row of double crochet (American single crochet) or for making appliqué decoration.

The fleece should not be washed as the fibres need to be greasy to cling together in spinning. The yarn produced can be washed afterwards, preferably after the crochet has been worked.

A spindle can be made from a wooden rod about 1·25 cm ($\frac{1}{2}$") in diameter and 25–30 cm (10–12") in length, with each end tapered to a smooth blunt point. The centre should be grooved all the way round to hold the end of wool securely without slipping.

To prepare the fleece for spinning, loosen the fibres gently by hand. Do not pull too hard as the loosened fibres must not be detached from the bundle of fleece. Pull out a sausage-like length of fibre and roll this well between the palms of the hands, and continue pulling and rolling the wool until a length of 25–30 cm (10–12") is obtained. Twist the end with the fingers and tie securely to the groove in the centre of the spindle.

Sit to the task, and roll the spindle against the left thigh with the palm of the right hand. The spindle should be turned in one direction only, towards the knee. This is more easily accomplished on a bare thigh as clothing tends to ruck. The wool coming from the fleece should be held firmly with the first finger and thumb of the left hand during spinning. Left-handed workers will naturally reverse all these directions.

The angle at which the yarn to be spun leads off the spindle is important.

121

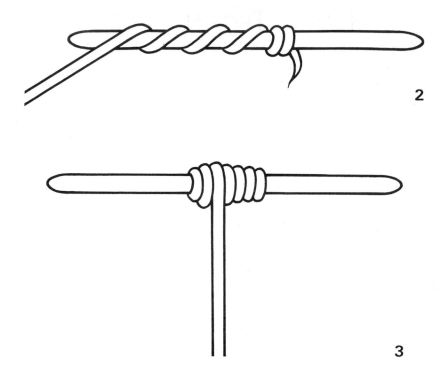

2

3

While the spindle is being rolled towards the knee, the yarn should lead off at an angle as shown in Figure 2. At the end of the action it will be wound several times around the spindle, as also shown in Figure 2. Now point the spindle in the direction of the left hand. This will allow the yarn wound round the spindle to slip off the end, and the total length of yarn will have been twisted.

Repeat these two actions till the yarn is judged to be sufficiently twisted. It should not be overtwisted or it will curl in knots. Now wind the spun yarn on to the centre of the spindle by holding it at a right angle to the spindle, as shown in Figure 3, while giving another roll on the thigh. It will now stay in place without slipping off the spindle. During the whole spinning and winding process, the thumb and first finger of the left hand should have kept a firm grip on the fibres coming from the fleece.

Using both hands, pull out another length of fibre from the fleece, again taking great care. Roll this between the palms of the hands, and repeat the process to spin a new length. *Figures 2 and 3, How to spin from hedgerow fleece.*

122

BASIC TECHNIQUES

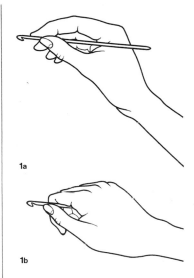

1a

1b

Figures 1a and 1b. Methods of holding the hook.

rochet is worked from one continuous thread, drawing one loop through another by means of a hook. There is only one loop or stitch on the hook at a time, so it is simple to control, and the notched head of the hook prevents the stitch from being dropped in error. The basic stitches are easy to learn but crochet does require practice to acquire the co-ordination necessary for even working. The directions which follow apply to right-handed workers. A note for left-handers is included later on p. 135.

How to Hold the Hook

There are two different ways in which the hook can be held. It can be wielded like a pen or like a knife.

The traditional method as shown in Figure 1a is suitable for light- or medium-weight yarns. Heavy or difficult yarns which require more pull on the hook can often be managed better if the hook is held as in Figure 1b. Use whichever method is the most comfortable. In either case, it is important to grip the hook as near to the notched head as possible as this gives a better control of work and the resulting crochet will have a more even appearance. If the hook cannot be held firmly, due to disability such as arthritis for example, then the shaft of the hook can be wrapped with foam rubber or any suitable padding well

123

strapped into position to give a better grip. In this case the hook is better held as in Figure 1b.

How to Hold the Yarn

Somehow a flow of yarn from its source at the ball has to be guided and fed to the hook, and at the same time it has to be controlled at an even tension. The manner in which this is achieved is immaterial, the only criterion being the finished appearance of the work. If the yarn flows too freely the stitches will be loose and uneven. If it does not flow freely enough the worker will become frustrated.

The traditional left-hand yarn hold allows a good development of speed in working, but the yarn can also be held in the right hand as generally used for knitting. The knit hold is slow by comparison but many beginners find it easier to manage, and prefer to master the stitches first and then to change to the quicker left-hand hold. Several variations are possible on the left-hand hold, and eventually a beginner will sort out a comfortable and personal way of handling. Either clutch the yarn with the first finger and thumb and guide with the second (Figure 2a), or interchange, and clutch with the second finger and thumb and guide with the first (Figure 2b). *Figures 2a and 2b. Interchange of first and second fingers.*

To control tension, the yarn can be wound on either the third finger or the fourth. Those who wear rings on the third finger will find it more con-

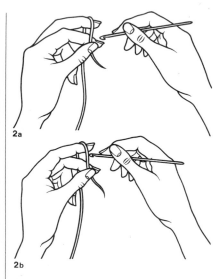

2a

2b

venient to wind for tension on the fourth. The yarn then ignores the third finger and can pass either over or under it (Figures 3a and 3b), and is wound in either direction on the fourth finger (Figures 3a and 3c). If the hands are warm it may not be necessary to wind the yarn for tension at all (Figure 3d). If the yarn is very silky and slithery it may need to be wrapped twice round the fourth finger (Figure 3e). *Figures 3a, b, c, d, e. Control of tension.*

How to Begin Work

A slip knot is needed to anchor the yarn to the hook. The advantage of a slip knot is that it can be pulled up to fit any size hook without being too bulky a knot. *Figures 4a, b, c, d. How to make a slip knot.*

The foundation or "cast-on" cro-

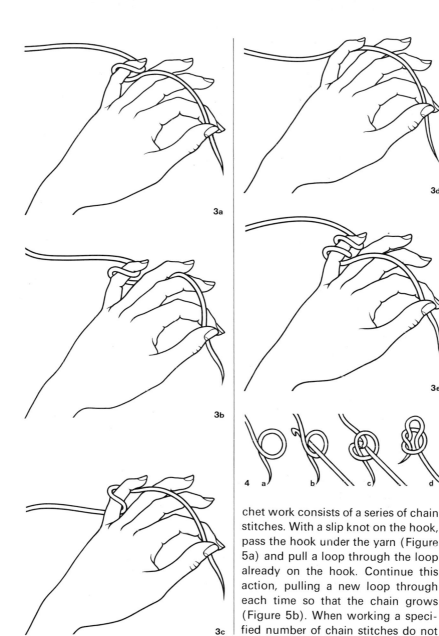

3a

3b

3c

3d

3e

4   a   b   c   d

chet work consists of a series of chain stitches. With a slip knot on the hook, pass the hook under the yarn (Figure 5a) and pull a loop through the loop already on the hook. Continue this action, pulling a new loop through each time so that the chain grows (Figure 5b). When working a specified number of chain stitches do not

125

count the slip knot which was originally on the hook, and if a re-count of the total is necessary afterwards do not include the loop on the hook. *Figures 5a and 5b. How to work a foundation chain.*

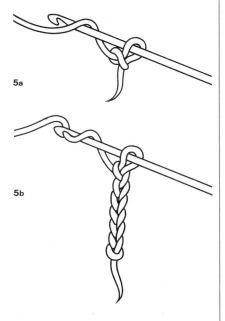

5a

5b

THE MAIN STITCHES

Double Crochet (American Single Crochet)

This stitch produces a close firm fabric. It is one of the most useful stitches, and is the one used most in the designs. Insert the hook from the front towards the back into the second chain from the hook (Figure 6a). Pass the hook under the yarn and draw a loop through the chain (Figure 6b). Pass the hook under the yarn again

and draw through both loops on the hook. The stitch is now complete (Figure 6c). Repeat this action into every chain to the end, being careful not to allow the foundation chain to twist. *Figures 6a, b, c. How to work double crochet (American single crochet).* Note that when inserting the hook into the foundation chain, it can be inserted either under one loop or under two loops of each chain. Either is correct providing work is consistent. If one loop is picked up from each chain, which is easier, two loops remain "unused". If two loops are picked up from each chain, which is neater but more difficult, one loop remains "unused". The latter edge will not have so much strength in wear as the former. Use whichever method is the most suitable for the article being made.

To work a second row, work one chain stitch with which to turn. This gives the work height ready for the next row. Turn the work sideways in order to work back in the opposite direction. Note that when working consecutive rows the hook is inserted under *both* loops of the stitch beneath. The turning chain is counted as the first stitch of the row, therefore insert the hook next into the second stitch missing the first. Then work into each stitch to the end. Do not miss the last stitch of the row which was the turning chain of the previous row.

The Treble (American Double Crochet)

126

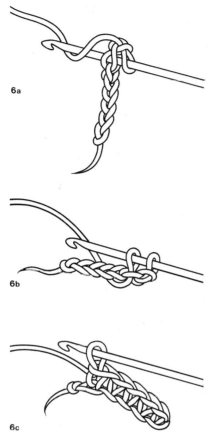

6a

6b

6c

This stitch does not produce such a close fabric as the double crochet (American single crochet). It is more than twice the height of the latter and consequently work grows more quickly.

Once double crochet (American single crochet) has been mastered, it is easier to continue working on the practice sample with a row of trebles (American double crochet), rather than start again with a new foundation chain. Before beginning a row of trebles (American double crochet), a turning chain of three chain stitches has to be worked in order to attain the height necessary for these stitches. The turning chain takes the place of the first stitch in a row.

To work a treble (American double crochet), pass the yarn over the hook first (Figure 7a). Hold the two loops now on the hook firmly in place with the first finger of the right hand, and insert the hook into the next stitch of the row beneath. Pass the hook under the yarn and draw through this stitch. There are now three loops on the hook. Pass the hook under the yarn (Figure 7b), and draw through two of the three loops. Again pass the hook under the yarn (Figure 7c) and draw through the remaining two loops. This completes the stitch (Figure 7d).

Continue working into each stitch to the end, working the last stitch into the top of the turning chain of the row beneath. *Figures 7a, b, c, d. How to work a treble (American double crochet).*

Note that when working trebles (American double crochet) it is especially important to remember that the turning chain counts as the first stitch of a row, and that the following stitch must be worked into the second stitch of the row beneath. Similarly, the last stitch of each row must be worked into the turning chain of the row beneath. Very strict attention must be paid to these details in order to keep the edges of the work straight.

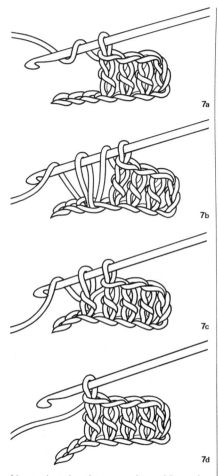

7a

7b

7c

7d

Note also that in normal working, the hook is always inserted under *both* top loops of the stitch in the row beneath.

Double Treble (American Treble)

The number of times that the yarn is passed over the hook before working a treble (American double crochet) can be increased to produce stitches of even greater height. The double treble (American treble) needs a turning chain of four chain stitches. To work a double treble (American treble), pass yarn-over-hook twice then insert the hook into the next stitch of the row beneath, pass hook-under-yarn and draw through the stitch. There are now four loops on the hook (Figure 8). Pass hook-under-yarn and draw through two of

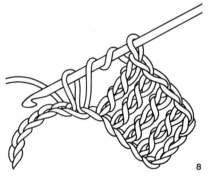

8

them, leaving three loops on the hook. Pass hook-under-yarn and draw through two loops again, so that there are two loops left on the hook. Repeat this action yet again, so that one loop is left on the hook. This completes the stitch. *Figure 8. How to work a double treble (American treble).*

Triple Treble (American Double Treble)

Pass yarn-over-hook three times,

128

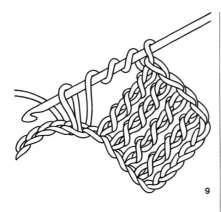

9

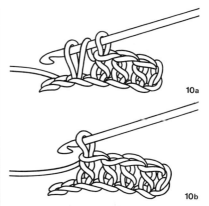

10a

10b

then insert the hook into the stitch beneath, pass hook-under-yarn and draw through the stitch (Figure 9). Pass hook-under-yarn and draw through two loops, four times. This completes a triple treble (American double treble). It requires a turning chain of five chain stitches. *Figure 9. How to work a triple treble (American double treble).*

Extremely long stitches can be produced by increasing the number of yarn-over-hook actions at the beginning. The extra loops on the hook are worked off in pairs in the same way as the triple treble (American double treble) is completed. Turning chains must be adjusted to a corresponding height.

Half Treble (American Half Double Crochet)

This stitch is half way in height between a double crochet (American single crochet) and a treble (American double crochet). It makes a firm fabric but is not such a popular stitch

as the latter as it is more difficult to work. Begin by passing yarn-over-hook once, insert the hook into the stitch beneath, pass hook-under-yarn and draw through the stitch (Figure 10a). Now pass hook-under-yarn and draw through all *three* loops at once (Figure 10b). This completes a half treble (American half double crochet). It requires a turning chain of two chain stitches. *Figures 10a and 10b. How to work a half treble (American half double crochet).*

Slip Stitch

The slip stitch is used mostly for joining other component parts of crochet work, and for decreasing at the beginning of a row. It is not usually used as a fabric stitch in its own right. To work a slip stitch insert the hook into the required place, pass hook-under-yarn (Figure 11) and draw through all the loops on the hook in one movement. This completes a slip stitch. *Figure 11. How to work a slip stitch.*

129

British and American Stitch Names with Abbreviations

British
chain (ch)
slip stitch (ss)
double crochet (dc)
half treble (halftr or htr)
treble (tr)
double treble (dbltr or dtr)
triple treble (triptr or trtr)

American
chain (ch)
slip stitch (ss)
single crochet (sc)
half double crochet (halfdc or hdc)
double crochet (dc)
treble (tr)
double treble (dbltr or dtr)

11

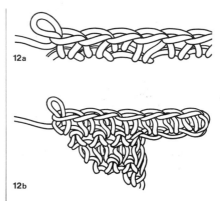

12a

12b

How to Finish Work

No "cast-off" is needed. Cut the yarn leaving an end sufficiently long to darn in, pass the hook under the end of yarn and draw the entire length through the last loop on the hook, pulling tightly.

How to Increase and Decrease in Crochet

There are many ways of shaping plain crochet fabric by increasing and decreasing the number of stitches. An obvious way to increase in crochet is to work two stitches into one of the previous row. Sometimes, however, this may be noticeable, and if a less noticeable effect is required, the second stitch can be worked into the back loop only of the stitch beneath (Figure 12a).

To increase several stitches at the beginning of a row, work additional chain to extend the work sideways (Figure 12b). The turning chain must still be allowed. *Figures 12a and 12b. How to increase.*

An obvious way to decrease is just to miss a stitch. This, however, may leave a noticeable gap in the fabric, and if this effect is not required, the method of avoiding a gap is to work two consecutive stitches together as one, rather like knit-two-together in knitting. In double crochet (American single crochet) this is achieved by inserting the hook into a stitch, hook-

130

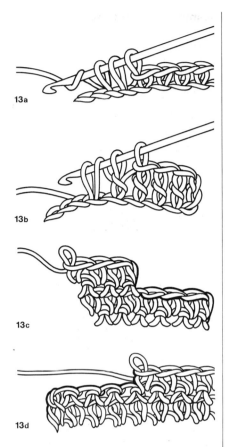

13a

13b

13c

13d

through two loops, pass yarn-over-hook and insert hook into the next stitch, hook-under-yarn and draw through (Figure 13b), hook-under-yarn and draw through two loops, hook-under-yarn and draw through three loops. This completes a treble (American double crochet) decrease.

To decrease several stitches at the beginning of a row, an equal number of slip stitches can be worked (Figure 13c). To decrease several stitches at the end of a row, merely turn before the end is reached (Figure 13d). *Figures 13a, b, c, d. How to decrease.*

How to Work Crochet in Rounds

Any of the basic crochet stitches can be worked in rounds, but the appearance will differ slightly from that of the same stitch worked in rows. This is because rounds which are worked in the same direction have a definite "right" and "wrong" side, whereas rows of the same stitch are reversible as they are worked in alternate directions. These differences in appearance need to be considered if the two techniques are combined in one article.

There are two methods of working rounds, one method forms a tubular coil of constant diameter, the other method forms a flat coil of increasing diameter. In both cases the rounds can be worked as a continuous spiral (Figure 14a), or each round can be joined individually (Figure 14b). *Figures 14a and 14b. Methods of working in rounds*

Method 14a, in which the rounds

under-yarn and draw through, insert the hook into the next stitch, hook-under-yarn and draw through. There are now three loops on the hook. Pass hook-under-yarn (Figure 13a) and draw through all three loops to complete the decrease. To decrease with trebles (American double crochet), pass yarn-over-hook, insert hook into a stitch, hook-under-yarn and draw through, hook-under-yarn and draw

131

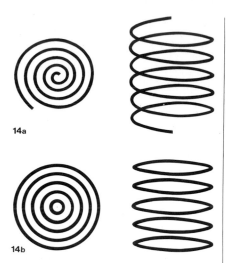

14a

14b

slip stitch into the far end of the chain (Figure 15a). Work eight double crochet (American single crochet), inserting the hook into the centre of the ring (Figure 15b). At this point decide whether to work spirally or whether to join each round separately with a slip stitch. The latter needs one chain before starting the following round. In either case, increase in the next round by working twice into

15a

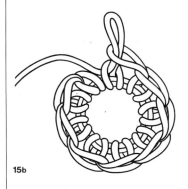

15b

are worked spirally, is a very easy technique, and can in effect be considered as one long round. It has the disadvantage that it ends abruptly with a "step" which needs tapering for a smooth finish. Any pattern or colour change used within the round will also show up as a "step".

Method 14b, in which the rounds are joined separately, has no "step" problem, but has the disadvantage that the join is usually visible unless disguised by pattern. Each round is joined with a slip stitch which connects the first and last stitches of the round, and a chain is needed to attain height before starting the following round.

To Work Flat Rounds of Double Crochet (American Single Crochet)

Start with a foundation of five chain and join into a ring by working

each stitch. The following time round, increase in every alternate stitch. Continue for the size required, increasing as necessary to keep the work flat. A safety pin or marker of coloured thread can be used to mark the original beginning of the round, and can be carried forward as work progresses. If working spirally, taper the finish of the final round by working two slip stitches before ending work. *Figures 15a and 15b. Working flat rounds of double crochet (American single crochet).*

To Work Tubular Rounds of Double Crochet (American Single Crochet)

Start with a foundation chain equal to the circumference of the rounds required, and make a ring by joining with a slip stitch, being careful not to allow the chain to twist. Work one double crochet (American single crochet) into each chain all round. At this point decide whether to work spirally or whether to join each round separately with a slip stitch. As before, the latter needs one chain before starting the following round. Work plain rounds without increasing for the size required. If working spirally, taper the finish of the final round by working two slip stitches before ending work.

How to Work Ridged Crochet

Each of the basic stitches has two loops at its top resembling a chain, and in normal work, whether of rows or rounds, the hook is always inserted under both top loops of the stitch in the row or round beneath. However, a ribbed or ridged effect can be produced if the hook is inserted under only one of these loops. Usually the back loop is chosen. Fabric worked in

this way has more stretch than fabric worked in the normal way, and the loops which remain "unused" on the front surface of the crochet form a continuous ridge of yarn.

Consecutive rows of double crochet (American single crochet) worked on the back loops are especially interesting as they take on a corrugated appearance. The method is not quite so striking when worked in rounds, but it does give a slight textural variation to some designs.

How to Work with Multiple Colours

Double crochet (American single crochet) lends itself especially well to a colour technique similar to the Fair Isle knitting technique. The method is only really practical when working in rounds, as the colours are carried across the back of the work when not in use, and it is too tedious to bring them all to the front and then reverse them again whenever rows are turned. However, when working in rounds, it is simple to handle two colours at once by winding one on the left hand and one on the right (Figure 16a). This keeps the yarns apart so that they do not tangle as they are apt to if used in turn on the same hand. With practice, four colours can be handled at once, two on each hand (Figure 16b). *Figures 16a and 16b. How to handle multiple colours.*

To introduce a new colour, just draw the new yarn through in place of the old, and cover the tail end of the new yarn by working over it when

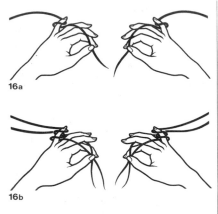

16a

16b

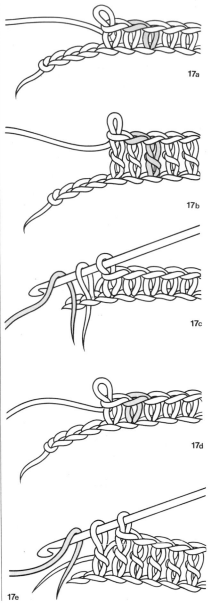

17a

17b

17c

17d

17e

working the next few stitches.

There are two ways of changing colour. One is to take on a new colour at the beginning of a new stitch. This sounds logical, but in practice the final draw through which completes the working of a stitch actually forms the top of the following stitch, so that the colours will "bleed" across (Figures 17a and 17b). If the colour design is intricate, this can be distracting, but if the colour design is simple, it adds interest.

The second method gives a clean-cut colour change. The new colour is taken on with the last draw through of the preceding stitch. Figures 17c and 17d show the method applied to double crochet (American single crochet). Figures 17e and 17f show it applied to trebles (American double crochet), and it can be applied to any other stitch similarly. *Figures 17a, b, c, d, e, f. Methods of changing colour.*

It is important that the colours not

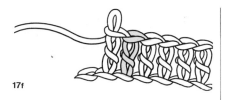

17f

in use which are carried across the back of the work should not be pulled too tightly. Practice will show how much sag to allow on the strands. The technique is mainly suited to short colour runs. If there is a long run of stitches between colour changes, it may be more practical to break the yarn.

How to Develop Speed in Working

Most beginners tend to use one hand more than the other, usually keeping the hand that holds the yarn fairly static and making all movements with the hand that holds the hook. It is possible to reverse this action, holding the hook static and making all movements with the other hand, literally throwing the yarn over the hook. Ideally both hands should interact, with an equal amount of movement from the wrist, and unless this is so, the worker will not acquire his or her potential maximum speed.

It is worthwhile trying to catch oneself unawares now and again, to see whether one hand is working more than the other. If so, try to develop more use of the lazy hand. On long rows it is also worth timing oneself to try and increase speed, but it often takes ten minutes or longer at a sitting before one can "warm up" and settle into a fast steady rhythm.

Crochet for Left-Handed Workers

Crochet needs the use of both hands, and for this reason left-handed beginners sometimes find the right-handed method acceptable. If it is not, then a left-handed worker holds the hook in the left hand and the yarn in the right.

The basic *written* directions for all stitches apply to right-handed or left-handed workers. Most left-handers have adapted to a right-handed world and are capable of translating diagrams mentally, but if necessary a mirror can be used to view the diagrams in reverse. A mirror will reverse the writing as well, so prop the book in such a way that diagrams can be viewed in the mirror and the directions read from the book at almost the same time.

How to Crochet with one Hand

Although two hands are required for working at speed, the loss of a hand is by no means a handicap. Perfect work can be achieved by a slower method. The hook needs to be clamped somehow as a replacement for the missing or useless hand, and all work is done by throwing the yarn over the static hook, using the one remaining hand whether right or left. A portable vice clamped to the top of a table is the answer to the problem. A right-handed worker should have the vice clamped to the left of the

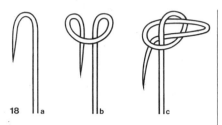

18 a   b   c

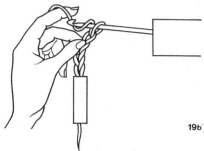

19b

body, and a left-handed worker should have the vice clamped to the right. The hook should be inserted into the jaws of the vice with a slight upward slant as shown, and the head of the hook should face at an angle of about 45° so that it faces the worker's eyes.

The most difficult part is the start. To make a slip knot, lay the yarn as an inverted U, bring the fold downward to form two loops, insert the fingers into one loop, pick up the other and draw through (Figures 18a, b, c), place the loop on the hook and tighten it. *Figures 18a, b, c. How to make a slip knot with one hand.*

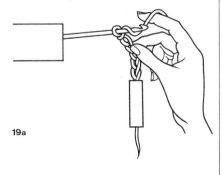

19a

The tail end of the yarn can be weighted with a clothes peg at first to provide stability. As work progresses the peg can be removed. The manner of handling the yarn is shown in Figures 19a and 19b. *Figures 19a and 19b. How to hold the yarn with one hand.*

MISCELLANEOUS FINISHES AND TRIMMINGS

Dealing with Ends

There is always a final tail end of yarn to be darned in and it should be cut long enough to be threaded into a needle for this purpose, but any other ends can be dealt with during working.

Knots, apart from the initial slip knot, are better avoided altogether if possible. Even manufacturer's knots in a ball of yarn are better taken out and the ends rejoined by splicing as explained in the chapter on Materials and Equipment (p. 120). Splicing is the ideal method of joining yarns but it is not suitable for joining different colours. In this case, the new end can

136

be laid along the top of the work and worked over so that it is enclosed by the following stitches (Figure 20). The old end can be laid with the new if necessary, but it is better if work permits to lay the old end in the opposite direction and to enclose it when working those stitches. *Figure 20. How to work over an end.*

20

An end of yarn at the beginning of work can often be used to sew a seam and sufficient should be allowed for the purpose. If it is not needed for seaming, then this end can be laid along the foundation chain and enclosed by the first row or the first round.

An end at the beginning of a flat round can be wrapped around the ring of chain and worked over when working the first round of stitches into the ring. If necessary, the aperture can be drawn in slightly by pulling on the end, before it is trimmed.

Methods of Seaming

There are several ornamental methods of seaming with the hook but the most useful method is the double crochet (American single crochet) seam. This is worked by inserting the hook through both layers of fabric to be joined, and working a double crochet (American single crochet). Re-peat for the length of the seam. It gives a very neat finish, but it is only suitable for smooth edges.

Edges which are in any way uneven or serrated are better sewn with a needle, by backstitching a little way in from the edge to smooth out the unevenness. If it is possible to do so, sew with a single ply or with half thickness of the yarn, as this will be less clumsy than sewing with full thickness. Not all yarns will divide in this way, some just disintegrate, but it is always worth trying.

There are several other methods of seaming crochet. A flat seam can be worked by weaving ladderwise from side to side with a needle. For extra strength, weave up the seam and then weave down the seam. An embroidered blanket stitch makes a good seam.

Drawstring Chains

These chains often need to be more substantial than foundation chains. A plain chain can be worked using double or triple thickness of yarn for strength, or an ornamental corded chain can be worked as follows.

Make a slip knot using a double thickness of yarn (Figure 21a), then thread one yarn on the right hand and the other on the left. Work a chain, using each yarn alternately (Figure 21b). This needs to be very evenly and closely worked and takes practice. Nor must the sequence of change be lost or the effect is spoiled. A double or triple thickness of yarn

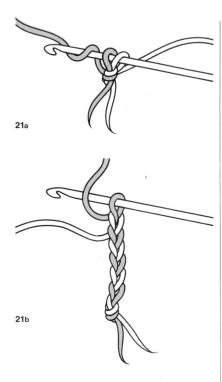

21a

21b

strong way of attaching ornaments, but has the disadvantage that the design must be planned in detail before beginning, as once in place the ornamentation is fixed.

An alternative method is to tie or sew each ornament on to the crochet fabric afterwards, and although this may not be considered so good technically, it allows much wider scope in planning, as the decoration can be moved around till a satisfactory design is achieved. The ornament can be sewn down closely or attached to hang loosely. Figure 22b shows how beads can be attached in pairs to hang loosely. The two ends of yarn

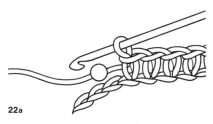

22a

can be used on each hand for a more substantial cord. *Figures 21a and 21b. How to make a corded chain.*

How to Attach Ornaments to Crochet

Beads, and indeed any ornament such as sequins, buttons or "found" objects, can be threaded on the ball of yarn before beginning work. Each bead or ornament is then slid into position at the back of the crochet fabric as required (Figure 22a), and work must be planned so that the back of the fabric is actually the front of the design. This is a very neat and

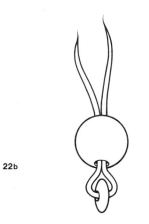

22b

are taken through to the back of the crochet fabric and securely tied or sewn. A series of mobile beads attached in this way can be very attractive. *Figures 22a and 22b. How to attach beads to crochet.*

Appliqué Crochet Motifs

Simple chains applied to a crochet fabric provide an easy means of decoration. A very similar appearance can be achieved by chain stitch embroidery, or by the tambour work technique of working a chain through the fabric, but again there is more scope in planning if the chain is worked separately and then arranged in an interesting design afterwards. Chains look especially attractive if applied face downwards to the crochet fabric, so that the rope-like back of the chain is displayed. An owner's initials can be added to an article in this way. The ends of yarn left at the beginning and end of each chain provide a means for sewing the chain into position, and they should be left sufficiently long for this purpose. Pin or tack the appliqué into position first.

Flat rounds of ridged double crochet (American single crochet) make good appliqué shapes, like little suns or full moons. They are worked spirally and the final end of yarn is used to sew them into position afterwards. Circles of different sizes and colours can be moved about the crochet surface at will before their positions are finally decided. The sewing need not necessarily be invisible. It can be a decorative embroidered addition to the design. There are no rules. Any technique is fair, and any ornament permissible, providing that it is a success in the context of the finished design.

BIBLIOGRAPHY

The following books encourage original design in crochet. The first three are especially concerned with uninhibited art school studies and exhibition works:

New Design in Crochet, Clinton D. Mackenzie, Van Nostrand Reinhold, 1972.

Creative Crochet, Nicki Hitz Edson and Arlene Stimmel, Watson-Guptill Publications, 1973.

The Crocheter's Art – New Dimensions in Free-form Crochet, Del Pitt Feldman, Nelson, 1975.

Crochet Techniques and Projects, Sunset Books, Lane Publishing Co., 1975.

Crochet by Design, Wynne Broughton, Pitman, 1976.

Illustrated Patchwork Crochet, Bella Scharf, Butterick Publishing, 1976.

Knitting and Crochet in Easy Stages, Eve de Negri, Studio Vista, 1977.

The following are collections of stitch patterns:

A Treasury of Crochet Patterns, Liz Blackwell, Pitman, 1972.

A Complete Guide to Crochet Stitches, Mary M. Dawson, Hodder and Stoughton, 1973.

The following are comprehensive needlework encyclopaedias with sections on crochet:

Encyclopaedia of Needlework, Thérèse de Dillmont, Dollfus-Mieg et Cie, (Mulhouse), first published 1886, English, French, Italian, German and Spanish editions.

Anchor Manual of Needlework, Batsford, 1958.

ACKNOWLEDGEMENT
To the Hand Crafts Advisory Association For The Disabled (Purley, Surrey), for permission to publish the technique of crochet with one hand.

INDEX